Prayerfully Yours

Prayerfully Yours

Brenda Poinsett

BROADMAN PRESS
Nashville, Tennessee

© Copyright 1979 • Broadman Press.

All rights reserved.

4282-55

Dewey Decimal Classification: 248.3

Subject heading: PRAYER

Library of Congress Catalog Card Number: 78-054776

Printed in the United States of America

*To
Carolyn, La Verne,
May, Ramona, Rosie,
and Violet.
Together we prayed,
and together we started asking questions
that needed answering.*

Unless otherwise noted, all Scripture quotations are taken from the King James Version of the Bible.

Scripture quotations marked TLB are taken from *The Living Bible.* Copyright © Tyndale House Publishers, Wheaton, Illinois, 1971. Used by permission.

Scripture quotations marked TEV are taken from *The Bible in Today's English Version.* Old Testament: Copyright © American Bible Society 1976. New Testament: Copyright © American Bible Society 1966, 1971, 1976. Used by permission.

Preface

The purpose of this book is to deal with misconceptions and problems that pray-ers have. These misconceptions and problems are worded as questions so they may be easily pinpointed and specifically answered.

The theme of the book is "It is right to ask." At first glance, the theme may appear too simple; but actually it is a profound and glorious truth. The theme does not overpower the purpose; rather, it serves as the thread which holds the garment together. Without thread, a garment would never serve its purpose, remaining always as separate pieces of material. Yet, for the most part, the thread remains unseen. The theme is not the prominent issue of each chapter, but it weaves the contents together to accomplish the book's purpose.

BRENDA POINSETT

Contents

1. Why Pray When God Already Knows What We Need? 11
2. Are Answers to Prayer Given to Those Who Possess Faith and Withheld from Those Who Do Not Have Faith? 18
3. Is There a Biblical Basis for "God Always Answers Prayer 'Yes,' 'No,' or 'Wait' "? 30
4. Is "Be Careful What You Pray for Because Your Prayers Might Be Answered" Biblically Sound Advice? 40
5. Is It Wrong to Beg God to Answer Our Prayers? 54
6. Should We Have Prayer Lists? How Long Should We Keep Someone or Something on the List? 64
7. When Is It Right to Put Out the "Fleece"? .. 72
8. Is It Wrong to Pray to Jesus or to the Holy Spirit? 80
9. What Does It Mean to Ask "in the Name of Jesus"? 90
10. Does God Answer the Prayers of Those Who Do Not Know Jesus? 100
11. Why Pray with Others? Isn't Praying Alone Enough? 112
12. What Is the Real Tragedy of Paul's Thorn in the Flesh? 120

1. Why Pray When God Already Knows What We Need?

Prayer is for asking. It is the way we bring our requests and needs to God. Jesus himself encouraged us to ask.

"*Ask*, and it shall be given you; seek, and ye shall find; knock, and it shall be opened unto you: For every one that *asketh* receiveth; and he that seeketh findeth; and to him that knocketh it shall be opened" (Matt. 7:7–8).

"And all things, whatsoever ye shall *ask* in prayer, believing, ye shall receive" (Matt. 21:22).

"And whatsoever ye shall *ask* in my name, that will I do, that the Father may be glorified in the Son. If ye shall *ask* any thing in my name, I will do *it*" (John 14:13–14).

"If ye abide in me, and my words abide in you, ye shall *ask* what ye will, and it shall be done unto you" (John 15:7).

"Whatsoever ye shall *ask* the Father in my name, he will give *it* you. Hitherto have ye asked nothing in my name: *ask*, and ye shall receive, that your joy may be full" (John 16:23–24).

Ask and *asketh* are italicized in these verses to show us how Jesus encouraged us to ask. But Jesus also said, "your Father knoweth what things ye have need of, before ye ask him" (Matt. 6:8). When we combine this statement with the others, we have a problem in understanding. Why pray when God already knows what we need?

Isn't God all-powerful, all-knowing, and all-loving? What is the point of asking something of a God who already knows everything and loves us unconditionally? Why doesn't he go ahead and do what he wants?

We must remember that God does give us many things before we ask. Many blessings come our way which we did not ask for, which we did not seek out in prayer. Further, it has been the delight of many Christians to find that when they did pray, the answer had already been prepared for them. "And it shall come to pass, that before they call, I will answer; and while they are yet speaking, I will hear" (Isa. 65:24).

When Jesus spoke the words "your Father knoweth what things ye have need of, before ye ask him," he was trying to correct some faults that had crept into the Jewish habits of prayer. Their prayers had become very repetitious like the pagans'. There was a kind of subconscious idea among them that if they battered long enough at God's door, he would answer. To them, God could be talked, and even pestered, into condescending to answer their prayers. So in effect, Jesus was saying, "You don't have to keep laying out your case before the one true God as the pagans pray to their gods. Why, God already knows what you need; so pray as if you know he does!"

But still we wonder, Why must we ask? If God already knows, why doesn't he just give us what we need? John Claypool answers this question by saying that there are some things God cannot give us unless we ask. Our salvation is an example. Jesus said, "Behold, I stand at the door and knock: if any man hear my voice, and open the door, I will come in to him, and will sup with him, and he with me" (Rev. 3:20). Jesus must be invited into our lives before he will enter. Asking is opening the door.

Our relationship with God, begun by opening the door to Jesus, is a personal one; therefore, God is not going to act on us impersonally. He does not regard us as blocks of wood to be sawed, shaped, and hammered into something. A carpenter may take a piece of wood and make out of it what he chooses. The wood has no feeling or will or intelligence to resist. If the carpenter wants to paint his created object red, he may do so. If he wants to paint it blue the next week, he can. The wood cannot resist the carpenter's efforts.

But personal relationships are not that way. There are many things that can only be given when there is a clear-cut willingness to receive. Claypool says that no matter how much power or desire a giver may possess, he cannot give if the recipient is unwilling and uncooperative. A graphic illustration of this is Jesus weeping over the Holy City and saying with a broken heart: "O Jerusalem, Jerusalem, . . . how often would I have gathered thy children together, as a hen *doth gather* her brood under *her* wings, and ye would not!" (Luke 13:34).

In the realm of the personal, some things can only be given when there is "an asking" that represents a desire to receive. Many parents have made the mistake of forcing blessings on their children when the children did not will to receive them. Sometimes this happens to parents who want to give their child a college education. They dream and work and plan for the day their child will enroll. They put money in a savings account; the mother takes a job outside the home. They bank her total salary to have enough to finance their child's education. But all of this time, the child has had other plans. The time comes for him to enroll. He says, "I'm not going." Enraged, the parents exclaim, "But you have to. We've planned and saved." The parents and the child become deadlocked into a battle of words as the giver insists on giving to an unwilling recipient.

How much different it would have been if, some time earlier in the child's life, he had said, "Mom, Dad, I want to go to college someday. I know it's going to be expensive and hard, but would you help me find a way?" Once the child asks, he has indicated his willingness to receive; and parents and child can work together to achieve what forcing could not achieve.

God will not force himself upon us. When we ask of God, all kinds of things become possible that never could have been possible before. Asking does not change or alter the purpose of God. What it does is give God an opportunity to do with and through us what he could never do to us or against us. God may see our need and may want to intervene, but he needs our willing hearts.

That asking indicates willingness, giving God a channel to work through us, answers our question about why we need to ask. But does it answer the needs of the person asking the question? The question reveals a lot about the prayer life of the questioner. It reveals a lack of experience in asking of God and a lack of knowledge of all that prayer is.

Only a person who has had little experience in asking of God would question the value of asking. The experienced asker may not know that asking indicates a willingness to receive, but he does know that asking brings relief. After talking a problem over with a dear friend who listens well, we conclude, "It helps just to talk about it," whether or not the friend offers any solution. We might say the same thing of God, for he *hears* prayers as well as answers them. And since he already knows all about us, he is not shocked by what we might ask for. When we go to him for that very thing which distresses us so much, our spirit will be refreshed by having asked. Our anxiety will disappear, and we'll be able to say, "It's worth the asking to gain the relief."

Jesus told us to ask that our joy may be full (John 16:24). Joy is the essence of Christianity, but it can be rounded out or made full (one translation says that our cup of joy may fill to the brim) by our asking of God and receiving. This completing of our joy is not to be equated with satisfaction in seeing a request answered. It goes beyond that, and it comes from having God repeatedly answer. Each time he does, God is saying, "I am alive. I do respond. I do care." Certainly there is joy in commitment, in forgiveness of sin, in the resurrection. But joy in these things reaches right up to the edge of our cup when God responds to our requests and confirms his reality.

Asking brings us relief and joy, and it brings God delight. Our asking can be a testimony to God. Asking expresses our faith; it shows God that we believe he can do anything. Our requests are a compliment to him and to his power and ability. A Christian may think he is doing God a favor by not asking, but he is really saying, "I do not believe you respond to me. I do not believe you are a God who hears and answers prayers." "The prayer of the upright is his [God's] delight" (Prov. 15:8), for each request expresses confidence in him, recognizing who he is and his ability to answer.

The person who asks the question "Why ask?" must look upon prayer as a means of getting. He must not know that prayer is also for thanksgiving and praise, confession, guarding against temptation, getting to know God, and aligning our wills with God's.

As God works and moves in our lives, we cannot ignore him. We feel compelled to respond, and prayer gives us a way to do it. We pray to say "Thank you" and "I'm grateful" and "I praise you." That's why we find prayer and thanksgiving inseparably linked together in the Bible. It was Paul's conviction that every prayer must include thanksgiving (Phil. 4:6; 1 Thess. 5:17-18; Col. 4:2).

Another feature of the majority of Bible prayers is the confession of sin they contain. A prayer like David's as recorded in Psalm 51 is stained with tears of repentance. After David's disastrous fall into sin he was cut off from fellowship with God, so he came to God with an honest confession of his evil thoughts and deeds. Fellowship was restored.

Prayer can also prevent the sin from occurring in the first place. When Jesus taught his disciples to pray "Lead us not into temptation, but deliver us from evil" (Matt. 6:13), he was trying to make them realize the kind of existence we have here on this earth and how we ought to live in the face of it. Jesus pictured this world as a battleground where opposing forces clash. Human strength is not enough up against "the principalities and powers" of evil. We can't kill the devil or demons by a sword, a gun, or physical force. None of these weapons would faze the devil or his agents. We need spiritual weapons, and prayer is one of them.

Part of the protection afforded us in prayer is the strength we derive from being in God's presence. Being alone with him and communicating with him refreshes us and enables us to know him in a personal, intimate way. To know him in a meaningful way, we must spend time with him; and prayer is an appropriate way to do that.

Prayer also enables us to align our wills with God's will. When we become Christians, we are saying, "I no longer know best for my own life. God does. I commit myself to doing what he wants." God's will is the standard. In prayer we lay our lives alongside that standard and pray until the two are one and the same. Prayer molds our wills to be in accordance with God's will.

Prayer is for thanksgiving, confession, protection, getting to know God, and will alignment. Most importantly, prayer is also for asking. We say "most importantly" because it is with asking that pray-ers have the most trouble. No one quibbles over the rightness of confessing or thanking, but much worry is spent over asking. "How do I know what to ask for without being selfish?" "Aren't there restrictions on what I can ask for?" "How many times must I ask?" "Can I bother God with trivia?" "How righteous must I be before God will readily grant my requests?"

We worry about these things because we've heard a lot of clichés and ideas about prayer that make asking sound very difficult—that we have to be holy and meet certain requirements and have impeccable faith, or God will not answer. What we have done with these ideas and clichés is boxed God in and said, "There's only one way in which God can work."

Well, it's time we let God out of the box. Let's examine those clichés and ideas about prayer for the truth that is in them. We'll study them not only in light of what the Bible says about prayer but in light of what the Bible shows us about God's response to pray-ers. We may be surprised at our findings. We just may discover that making sure we ask is more important than how we ask. We may be surprised to discover how much God needs our asking as a clear indication of our willingness to receive.

2. Are Answers to Prayer Given to Those Who Possess Faith and Withheld from Those Who Do Not Have Faith?

Much time is spent among Christians trying to find the keys to a faith that will never waver and will produce outstanding results. Nowhere is this more true than with regard to prayer. There's a hunt on for a formula that will guarantee answers. The belief is that answers to prayer are given to those who possess faith.

Answered prayer is related to faith. The Bible gives us too many promises and too many examples linking faith and answered prayer for us to think otherwise.

"All things, whatsoever ye shall ask in prayer, believing, ye shall receive" (Matt. 21:22).

"And Jesus answering saith unto them, Have faith in God. For verily I say unto you, That whosoever shall say unto this mountain, Be thou removed, and be thou cast into the sea; and shall not doubt in his heart, but shall believe that those things which he saith shall come to pass; he shall have whatsoever he saith. Therefore I say unto you, What things soever ye desire, when ye pray, believe that ye receive them, and ye shall have them" (Mark 11:22–24).

"Jesus said unto him, If thou canst believe, all things are possible to him that believeth" (Mark 9:23).

"And the Lord said, If ye had faith as a grain of mustard seed, ye might say unto this sycamine tree, Be thou plucked up by the root, and be thou planted in the sea; and it should obey you" (Luke 17:6).

"But let him ask in faith, nothing wavering. For he that wavereth is like a wave of the sea driven with the wind and tossed. For let not that man think that he shall receive any thing of the Lord" (Jas. 1:6-7).

These verses present clear evidence that answers to prayer and faith are related. The solution to having prayers answered is to have faith. All we need to do is produce the faith, and we'll have the answers. No problem with that—or is there?

There is. At least, there is for many of us. Producing mountain-moving, tree-uprooting faith is not easy; but it can be done if we are willing to follow some simple suggestions. We'll call these suggestions faith-builders because they are things we can do to increase our faith and thereby increase our answers to prayer requests. Faith is sometimes given to us. But faith is also a matter of the will, the mind, and the actions of the believer which are what these faith-builders are concerned with.

1. *Pray aloud.* This suggestion may appear to be ridiculously simple, but to those of us still praying with our thoughts alone, praying aloud can be a real breakthrough. It's not that God will not answer thought prayers; but praying aloud will increase our faith, and that's what we are concerned about.

Voicing our petitions in a clear, audible manner when we are alone affirms the reality of God; we're talking to someone who really exists! We can better present our needs and be more in control of our prayer. With our thoughts, it is easy to drift in and out of prayer, making it difficult to distinguish random thinking from praying. Voicing the requests lessens our timidity and assures us that we have indeed presented the requests to someone who can do something.

2. As we pray aloud, we should *make prayer a real conversation*, using our natural, ordinary conversational voice. Switching to the language of the King James Version of the Bible will stifle our praying because we are expressing ourselves in an unnatural way. Some Christians have prayed using *thees* and *thous* for so long that it seems natural to them. They pray quite well that way, but they might be surprised at what else they might say if they used their everyday language.

Praying in our conversational voice doesn't mean God does not hear prayers uttered in a holy tone or sprinkled with *thees* and *thous*. God hears prayers, but it is our faith-praying that we are concerned about. We'll be more confident in expressing ourselves when we are doing it naturally.

Any conversation involves two, so we need to imagine that Christ is present and that we are actually speaking with him. We need to politely pause and let him speak to us. The reality of Christ's presence and his response will encourage us and increase our faith.

3. These conversations will be enhanced and strengthened if we *establish a regular time and place* for them. Praying regularly eliminates praying only when we feel like it. When we pray regularly at a set time, we are acting on the fact that God hears and answers prayer, not on whether we feel like praying. Keeping that set time with God can make all the difference when we are discouraged or when God seems to have removed his presence from us. Our faith grows as we experience him during those moments when we make ourselves pray, and we learn through regular contact how unchanging and supportive God is.

A definite place to pray isn't necessary, but having one helps us keep our appointed time. We can look upon the spot as a place for spiritual refreshment, being reminded of what awaits us there every time we pass it. We can keep our Bible there and other devotional aids to use along with our prayer-conversations.

4. *Join a prayer group.* Hearing others pray, listening to how they voice their petitions, and noting what they ask for will increase our own boldness in praying. As we meet with them on a regular basis, we see God answering. Those answers can be a boost to our faith.

Not having the time keeps many Christians from joining a prayer group. Prayer with one other person does not involve quite the same amount of time; yet the joy of claiming his presence and his promise to answer where two or three gather together can still be claimed. That's a promise no Christian should want to miss out on, and we'll see why when we get to chapter 11.

5. Asking for a mountain to be removed will do nothing for our faith unless we really believe God will do it. It is better to pray, asking for what we really believe God will do. Rosalind Rinker says to *use faith-sized requests.* A faith-sized request is a request for a particular situation in which we pray for a special person or thing, asking only for that which we believe God will do. Whenever we start to pray for something we should ask ourselves, *Do I really believe God will grant it?* If we don't, we should whittle the request down until it is the right believing size for our faith.

One way to do this is by trying to picture receiving the answer. Ask, *Can I picture myself receiving this answer as I have prayed for it?* If we can't, that may be an indication that we don't really believe God will answer. We need to change our request until we can picture receiving the answer—until it is the right size for our faith.

Asking for smaller things doesn't sound like faith building, but in practice it is. As our faith grows through receiving answers to smaller requests then we will be encouraged to ask for more and larger things.

6. As we present our faith-sized requests, we can *thank God for the answer* before we receive it. Thanking God before the evidence of his answer is in hand has been an aid to the faith of many praying Christians, but I have found the step difficult. In theory, I believe it; but practicing believingly and confidently has not been easy. I find myself having to slide into using it. "God, I thank you that even now you are working to answer my request." Daniel 10:12 helps me do that. When the man from God appeared to Daniel in a vision he said, "Fear not, Daniel: for from the first day that thou didst set thine heart to understand, and to chasten thyself before thy God, thy words were heard, and I am come for thy words." The man of God had been detained for twenty-one days, *but* Daniel's prayer had been heard immediately. That I can handle! And so I pray, "I thank you that you are hearing my prayer and you are beginning now to answer."

7. Sometimes instead of actually thanking God, I talk to him about Daniel's experience. I say, "I remember how you immediately heard Daniel's prayer. I'm expecting you to hear mine right now and to begin to take action to work out the answer." Now, God doesn't need to be reminded of his action regarding Daniel. I am the one who needs the reminder, so *I use examples of answered prayer from the Bible or quote prayer promises from the Bible* when I pray.

Some good prayer promises to memorize and quote are found at the beginning of this chapter. Others include

Matthew 7:7-8; 21:21; John 14:13-14; 15:7,16; 1 John 5:14-15. Memorizing these verses and quoting them in our prayers help convince us that these promises are indeed ours to claim.

We can't quote these examples or promises from the Bible unless we know they are there. That's one reason why our Bible needs to be a part of our set time and place for prayer.

8. We should *remove expressions of doubt* from our prayers. Saying doubtful things in our prayers plants doubt in our minds. Doubt is the biggest enemy of faith.

One such expression of doubt is "if it be thy will." John Bisagno says, "No prayer, to be a perfect prayer of faith, can contain the expression: if it be thy will!" Bisagno says pray-ers use "if it be thy will" as an escape clause. We do not really believe God is going to do what we ask, so when he doesn't, we can say, "Well, evidently it must not have been God's will." [1] Nothing about the phrase indicates belief and confidence on our part, which is what we are trying to raise by increasing our faith. We need to state our requests in a positive manner, nurturing our faith rather than hindering it.

9. Our faith can also be nurtured if we *use our imagination.* Doubt is at work in our minds, so why not use the wonderful imagination God has given us to work against it?

—Imagine Christ's presence. In our set place where we pray, we can picture his presence by creating a bodily shape with our minds and holding it in position as we pray. If our set place to pray is in the living room, we can picture Christ sitting at the other end of the couch or in a nearby chair. My personal preference is to sit at the kitchen table and imagine Jesus sitting in a chair across the table from me.

With that mental image in place, we direct our conversation toward him. Jesus is there; he is real; he is listening. We pour out our hearts to him as we would to a dear friend. We slow down, we pause, because someone is really there; and that someone may want to respond. A mental picture of Christ's presence helps us believe that two parties really do participate.

—Another kind of picture we may create is one of the burden for which we are praying. With our hands, palms up, in front of us, we picture the burden we are praying for in much the same way we might hold a basketball or a bowl of fruit. As we talk to the Lord about the burden, we see it before us; and we sense its heaviness. When we have told him all about it and what we expect him to do with it, we hand the burden to him (extend the hands upward or across the table to wherever his imagined presence is). This action helps us turn the burden over to him instead of carrying it with us after we pray. Closing the door firmly as we leave our set place of praying can accomplish the same thing.

—Faith results from being overwhelmed by God's love, but the problem is that we don't always feel loved, let alone overwhelmed by love. Again, our imagination can help. Rosalind Rinker suggests imagining a conversation with ourselves with both sides of the dialogue coming out of our mouths.

> *Mary:* Lord Jesus, are you right here with me?
> *Jesus:* Yes, Mary, I am here with you.
> *Mary:* Your love for me never changes, does it?
> *Jesus:* No, my love for you never changes; I always have and I always will love you.
> *Mary:* But Lord, sometimes I'm a mighty mixed-up person. How can you love me? Most of the time I don't even like myself.
> *Jesus:* I understand how you feel. Your insight about yourself

is indeed limited. I, however, love you for yourself, and
my love includes your total self—your *real* self, and all of
your potential. Believe this, for I am here to help you.[2]

—A similar way in which we can use our imagination to help us believe God loves and cares for us is to imagine ourselves in the position of someone who approached Jesus—the woman at the well, a child, the woman who touched the hem of his garment, or Jairus, a synagogue ruler. As we imagine ourselves in their situations, we can see and feel how Jesus regarded their needs.

Often I have been helped by substituting myself in the place of the leper in the account in Matthew 8:1-5. As the leper approached Jesus, he said, "Sir, if you want to, you can heal me" (TLB). How did Jesus react? First, he touched him. Think of what his touch meant to a leper. But it's what Jesus said to him that means so much to me. He said, "I want to. Be healed" (v. 3). When doubt strikes me as to whether God would do what I am about to ask, I recall the leper's experience. I say, "God, if you want to, you can . . ." And then I hear his answer, "I want to, Brenda; I want to." How those words encourage me to go ahead with my petition.

These four simple little exercises of the imagination help us eliminate our doubt and help us believe God really does love and care for us. It's a matter of mind over the devil.

As we worked through these faith-builders, who or what was the object we intended to change—God or us? Did we change God in any way? Did we alter his promises? Did we make the requirement of faith less stringent? No, our intent was to change ourselves—to increase our faith. What we attempted to change about ourselves was our approach to God, the way we ask him about matters that concern us. We worked on the climate of our asking (having a real conversation with God, alone and with others, at a set time and place). We taught ourselves how to improve our asking by editing what we actually say to him: using faith-sized requests, giving thanks before the answer, quoting from the Bible, and removing expressions of doubt. We can control our minds through our imagination to believe God will respond to our asking. The climate in which we pray, what we say, and what we think are all important. They affect our asking, and asking is what we must do if we are to exercise our faith and receive the results.

As we practice these faith-builders, we're going to experience answers to prayer requests. We'll prove in our lives what the Bible says is true: Faithfulness is rewarded. Answers to prayer are given to those who possess faith. But can we turn the statement around? Can we say that if we do not possess faith, we do not receive answers to prayer? Are answers withheld from those who do not have faith?

Just as the Bible gives us promises concerning faith and answered prayer, it also shows us how faith works. Let's look at a series of examples in the life of Jesus to see if faith or a lack of it makes a difference. Mark 4:35 through 6:6 records a series of happenings in which we see Jesus attempting to meet people's needs.

Jesus calmed the wind and the sea when the disciples were frightened by the sudden storm. Then he asked them, "How is it that ye have no faith?" (4:40).

The Gadarene demoniac did not seek Jesus for deliverance; Jesus acted in his own power under his own initiative. The only evidence of faith we can see in the demoniac was his acknowledgment of who Jesus was.

Faith does act in the next two stories. A shy, timid woman who trembled in the presence of Jesus summoned all her courage to touch the hem of his garment. Today we would hardly describe her manner of action as mountain-moving faith; yet Jesus said to her, "Thy faith hath made thee whole" (5:34).

Jairus, a synagogue ruler, defied his background and came boldly to Jesus. We know his faith was important because when the news came that Jairus' daughter had died, Jesus said, "Be not afraid, only believe" (5:36).

Jesus did not do the same mighty works in his hometown of Nazareth (6:5). What was the difference? Why could he not work in Nazareth as he did in the lives of these other people? The amounts of faith held by the disciples, the demoniac, the woman, and Jairus were not the same; and in some cases there was none. Why did Jesus work in their lives and not in the lives of the citizens of Nazareth?

The citizens of Nazareth regarded Jesus as Mary's son, not the son of God. They did not acknowledge who he was. The commitment of the disciples to follow Jesus shows they believed in him even if their faith was not all it should be. As tormented as the demoniac's mind was, he still recognized Jesus. The woman's faith was not as bold as Jairus', but she knew that Jesus had the ability to help her. Jesus works in the lives of those who acknowledge who he is.

The writer of Hebrews says that the faith which pleases God must consist of two things. We must believe that he is and that he rewards our seeking him (11:6). Our asking, our stating our request, says to him, "I acknowledge you. I believe you are real. I believe you will respond or I wouldn't ask."

William B. Coble, Midwestern Baptist Theological Seminary professor, defines faith as that thing in man which allows God to work in his life. The citizens of Nazareth would not allow God to work in their lives. The power, which they didn't recognize, was there in their midst; but they did not will to receive it.

We must will to receive what God has to offer. The faith-builders will help us to do that. Our quest is not to get a certain amount of faith to ensure answered prayers. Our quest is to become willing to receive all that God already wants to give us.

Sometimes, however, certain faith-builders have been such a breakthrough for us that we are tempted to put our faith in the builders instead of in the God who answers prayer. We deceive ourselves into thinking we have found *the* formula for getting answers. A little smugness develops. We look at others suffering along with their unanswered requests and think, *Surely they must not have faith. If they did, God would grant their requests as he grants mine.* (See the implication: God withholds answers from those who do not have faith.)

Helen Good Brenneman is a prominent and prolific Mennonite writer and a frequently sought speaker. She also has multiple sclerosis. Although she is confined to a wheelchair and her vision is seriously impaired, she continues to write and speak. She says one of the great trials of her affliction is

> when well meaning friends suggest that lack of faith on the part of my husband, Virgil, and I is the obstruction that blocks my healing. Letters and telephone calls, personal visits from friends like those of Job, gently or harshly suggest (even insist) that miserly faith on our part stops God from doing this work of grace in my life.[3]

This same accusation that was hurled at Mrs. Brenneman also appears in some literature that we read on prayer. Here's the gist of their message: "If you ever hear people say they have trusted God or they had faith about a matter and still did not get it, you may be assured that they did not really have faith." The law is that God answers prayer. When he doesn't, something is wrong with our faith.

God does indeed answer prayer. It is his nature to answer prayer, but to say a no answer indicates a lack of faith on our part denies God's wisdom in answering. We can ask for something which is perfectly right for Christians to possess and ask with mountain-moving faith, and God still may answer no. His perspective is different from ours. His timing is different. His intention for us may be entirely different from how we perceive ourselves. Out of his perfect love and perfect wisdom, he must choose to do other than what we ask for our sake and for his.

Answered prayer and faith are related—so much so that we can work to build our faith to receive all that God wants to give us. Our confidence, however, should not be in the amount of faith we possess. No certain amount guarantees an answer. Neither can we say that a no answer means a lack of faith. In the next chapter, we'll see how God responded to the faith of pray-ers in the Bible. Let's see if there was a lack of faith on the part of the pray-ers that caused God to say no.

Notes

1. John Bisagno, *The Power of Positive Praying* (Grand Rapids: Zondervan Publishing House, 1972), p. 18.
2. Rosalind Rinker, *Communicating Love Through Prayer* (Grand Rapids: Zondervan Publishing House, 1966), p. 105.
3. Quoted in Robert J. Baker, *God Healed Me* (Scottsdale: Herald Press, 1974), p. 42.

3. Is There a Biblical Basis for "God Always Answers Prayer 'Yes,' 'No,' or 'Wait' "?

Our language is full of clichés. Many of us would have difficulty speaking if we had to eliminate them from our conversations. We use clichés because we have heard others use them regardless of whether we know their origin or meaning. In the expression "robbing Peter to pay Paul," who were Peter and Paul? (The answer is not Peter and Paul of the Bible.) Where was "the handwriting on the wall" written, and what did it say? "The grass roots" originally referred to a political party, but that doesn't keep any of us from using it when talking about basics. No knowledge of origin or meaning is necessary to confidently use a cliché.

A cliché often used by Christians is "God always answers prayer yes, no, or wait." Originally, it was probably an imaginative and forceful expression, but it has become weak through overuse. It is written in books on prayer; it is offered as advice in a syndicated religious newspaper column; it is printed on a bookmark of principles of prayer distributed by a widely circulated religious magazine.

Because it is easier to say what someone else has said than to go to the Bible to see what God really did do, we repeat, "God always answers prayers yes, no, or wait." It could be that the statement is not altogether true. Let's find out by seeing what the Bible reveals about God's answers to prayer.

The nature of the cliché suggests that something was asked for, so we need to examine those prayers in the Bible in which a specific request was made. If the request wasn't specific, we would have no way of measuring the answer.

The research is simple in form: go through the Bible and list the Bible reference, the prayer request, and God's answer. I charted my research, penciling those three items in columns. Then with a red felt-tipped marker I wrote yes, no, or wait beside God's answer. Before I was through Exodus, I was already feeling that the cliché was a little trite to describe the way God answers. The exercise of seeing what God really did do was a beautiful experience. I was thrilled to see how God responded to man's requests. He answered with understanding; he answered quickly; and he answered yes. My husband, walking by my desk, stopped to glance at my chart. "Didn't God ever answer no?" he asked.

The yes answers are many—too many to list here. They would make a fantastic book in themselves: *The Great Yes Answers in the Bible* or *The Readiness of God to Answer Yes.* Herbert Lockyer has authored a book that records all the prayers of the Bible and offers a commentary on each one. From his study, Lockyer says, "From Genesis to Malachi we have ample proof of prayer being fully answered by God. No sincere saint was sent away empty. No petition in submission to the divine will failed of an appropriate answer." [1] In the New Testament we see the same kind of response from Jesus as he listened to people's requests and met their needs. The evidence that God answers and answers quickly is further confirmed in the prayers of the early Christians as recorded in Acts.

Wait answers are hard to find. Abraham's prayer for

an heir would probably be one. God had promised Abraham that he would make of his descendants a great nation, but Abraham got weary in waiting for the son that would make this possible. In Genesis 15:2–5 Abraham questioned God concerning his promise. The heir still was not given, *but immediate reassurance was.* God promised Abraham he would have a son, his own son, as his heir. God took Abraham outside into the darkness and said, "Look up . . . . count the stars if you can. Your descendants will be like that" (TLB). From then on, when Abraham got discouraged in his waiting, he had only to look at the stars to be reminded of God's promise.

Another wait answer also concerns the birth of a child, although the Bible does not record the specific request being made. We assume that Zacharias prayed for a son because the angel appearing to him in the temple said, "Fear not, Zacharias: for thy prayer is heard; and thy wife Elisabeth shall bear thee a son" (Luke 1:13). How much earlier that prayer was made we do not know, so we have no idea how long Zacharias might have waited for his request to be answered.

Other than these two examples, wait answers to specific requests are hard to find. In 1 Samuel 14:37 there is a reference concerning God's not answering the day the prayer was prayed. Daniel once had to wait twenty-one days for a prayer to be answered. Jeremiah waited ten days. We sense waiting in the confessional or lamenting type of prayer (see Ps. 22:1–2; 40:1; 80:4; 88:14; and Hab. 1:2). Waiting for God to answer is a biblical implication, but not one to be confirmed in the answers to specific prayer requests.

The no answers are interesting. Since they are few in number, let's take a look at them.

Almost half of the no answers are given to men who

prayed to die. Number 11 records Moses praying to God to kill him. Under the burden he carried, Moses gave in to his feelings. Disgusted with divinely provided manna, the people longed for the delicacies of Egypt. They forgot the brick kilns, the task masters, and the sting of the whip. The accumulation of their complaints wearied and discouraged Moses, so he prayed to die. God did not just answer no. He said, "No, I'll give you help instead. I'll give you seventy men to help carry your burden" (Num. 11:16, author's paraphrase).

Other Old Testament men prayed for death, too. In his misery, Job prayed to die, a prayer easy to understand under his circumstances. Judging by the end of Job's life, God's answer to Job seemed to be, "No, I'll not let you die; I am not finished with you yet. There are more trials to come, true; but afterward many blessings await you." Job 42:12 reads, "And the Lord blessed the latter days of Job more than his beginning."

After Elijah's victorious stand against Baal, he fled from the wrath of Jezebel and requested to die (1 Kings 19:4). But God refused Elijah's request. "Had God granted the prophet's desire to die, his earthly ministry would have missed its crowning and unique glory" of being taken to heaven by a chariot and horses of fire in a whirlwind.[2] Who would have wanted to miss something like that?

Jonah too despaired and wanted to die. Jonah was upset because God canceled his plans to destroy Nineveh; he wanted God to confine his love and mercy to Israel. The Bible does not tell us if Jonah's prayer was answered, but we assume it wasn't by the care God used in making Jonah see the error of his thinking. Lockyer says, "How infinitely kind and gracious God is! With a mother's sweet gentleness He asked: 'Doest thou well to be angry?' Then with exquisite kindness God took special loving care of

His tired servant. God did not chide Jonah, but comforted him."[3] He gave Jonah an object lesson through a gourd that grew up quickly, gave Jonah shelter, and disappeared quickly when attacked by a worm. God used the plant to make Jonah feel something of his own pity for men and women.

God was not giving in to the despair of men when he answered no to the death wishes of Moses, Job, Elijah, and Jonah. He had a better way of dealing with their desires than giving them what they asked for.

David's request for the child of his and Bathsheba's shame to live was denied. As in the answer to Moses, we see God acting mercifully. If the child had lived, he would have been a perpetual reminder to David of his sin. Another son came in whose birth was no hint of shame.

In both the cases of Moses and David, for God to have answered their prayers in the way they were asked, he would have had to ignore the disobedience in their lives. His answer to them was not just no, but no with mercy. There's a difference!

Despair or sin wasn't always involved when the answer was no. The healed Gadarene demoniac had an intense desire to follow Jesus and be with him. The King James Version of the Bible records the healed demoniac as praying to Jesus to take him with him (Mark 5:18). His desire was a noble one, but Jesus said "No, go home to your friends," he told him, "and tell what wonderful things God has done for you" (vv. 19–20, TLB). In essence, Jesus was saying to him, "You become my preacher in this community. I have to go away now, but I'll be back. When I come back and find fruit from your work, that will be worth more to me than if you were allowed to become my constant companion." The next time that Christ came to that community, thousands of people welcomed him, for it was there that he fed the five thousand men plus women and children. It was in the same place where he had said no to the restored demoniac about devoting his life selfishly and commanded him to witness to others.

The two most poignant no answers are the answers given to Jesus' request for the cup of suffering to be removed and Paul's request for the thorn to be removed. Both Paul and Jesus placed their request three times; both involved suffering. In both cases, God answered no.

Now, what if God had answered his only son's request yes? Where would we be? Jesus' request had to be denied for a greater purpose to be served. Need more be said about the rightness of that no answer?

God did not answer Paul's request as he prayed it, but God did give him the grace to live with the thorn. Of all the answers to prayer in the Bible, including the yeses, none have probably helped Christians more through the years than the answer God gave to Paul. "My grace is sufficient for thee: for my strength is made perfect in weakness" (2 Cor. 12:9).

From these no answers that we've examined, we see God answering in tenderness and understanding. He does not succumb to man's despair in order to answer yes. Neither does he ignore sin, but he deals mercifully with the sinner. He answers from a different perspective. He thinks of all men rather than of the petitioner only. Neither will he answer no unless he gives the pray-er the grace to bear his situation. If the yes answers of the Bible don't encourage us to pray, then the nos should!

"God answers prayer yes, no, or wait" seems a little glib to describe the way God answers, although so far in our research we see him doing exactly that. But our research shows more about the way God answers. The

Bible shows us that God responds in ways other than yes, no, or wait.

At times pray-ers simply sought God's direction (which way to go or what to do), and the answer was given. After Joshua's death, the Israelites asked the Lord, "Which of our tribes should be the first to go to war against the Canaanites?" God answered, "Judah" (Judg. 1:1-2, TLB). We see this same kind of seeking direction in Judges 20. The Israelites asked, "Which tribe shall lead us?" (v. 18, TLB). "Shall we fight further?" (v. 24, TLB). "Shall we . . . fight . . . or shall we stop?" (v. 27, TLB). Each question was answered by God.

One could say that since direction was given, we should classify those answers as yes answers. That's partially what's wrong with using the cliché. It keeps us from seeing how God responds, how he listens, how he answers individually according to the situation. Prayer is not just for getting something, as the answers of yes, no, or wait imply. Prayer is communication. "Moses said unto God," and "God said unto Moses." "Samuel said," and "the Lord said." "Abram heard the Lord say," "But Abram answered," and "Then he heard the Lord speaking again" We talk to God and he talks to us.

Sometimes prayers were answered differently than requested, while still meeting the need of the pray-ers. One example is recorded in Numbers 21:7-9, in which Moses prayed for the removal of the serpents in their midst and for the avoidance of evil. God instructed Moses to make a bronze serpent and set it on a pole. If a man were bitten by a serpent, he could look upon the bronze serpent and live. God did not remove the serpents, but he did provide a remedy for those bitten.

At times God's response exceeded that of the petition. Solomon asked for wisdom, and God's answer included wisdom, riches, honor, and long life (2 Chron. 1:7–12). We don't know exactly how Peter's friends were praying for him while he was in prison, but they were very surprised when he appeared at their prayer meeting (see Acts 12). Paul says that God can do much more than we can ever ask or even think of asking.

The Bible also shows us that our relationship with God is a personal one. We can see this in God's responses to the prayers to die uttered by Moses, Job, Elijah, and Jonah. In each case the request was the same, but the answer was not. If they had all been answered in the same way, that would mean that God looked upon all of them in the same way, denying the personal relationship he had with each man. God responds uniquely to each of us. He knows us by name and not by number.

In one sense there is a biblical basis for "yes, no, or wait," but the total picture from the Bible shows there's so much more to God's responses. The cliché is true, but there is not enough truth in it. It doesn't begin to describe the greatness of God and his generous response to our prayers. God's answers express great wisdom and great love. The pray-ers of the Bible knew God responded to men; they expected him to answer. "I will climb my watchtower now, and wait to see what answer God will give to my complaint" (Hab. 2:1). God did not disappoint their expectancy.

Knowing how God answers, with great understanding and wisdom and with regard to our individual uniqueness, should do two things for us.

First, it should encourage us to ask. "Yes, no, or wait" repeated over and over begins to give us the impression that we have a chance of one in three of getting what we want. The Bible itself records approximately ten yes answers for every no, but even that should not be our incentive to pray. Praying is not a matter of getting what we want, but a matter of presenting our case to God for him to decide what is best. We can ask with every confidence, knowing that the right and appropriate thing will be done. We can ask even when there has been disobedience in our lives because we know he will deal with us mercifully. We can ask, knowing that if he refuses, he will give us his grace. We can ask because the Bible shows us he will answer.

Secondly, knowing how God answers should discourage us from repeating "God always answers prayer yes, no, or wait." We should especially restrain ourselves from repeating it to someone who has experienced a no answer to prayer. What made me start questioning the biblical basis for this cliché was seeing the crestfallen looks on people's faces who were dealing with no answers as a fellow Christian would prattle to them, "God always answers prayer yes, no, or wait." "This is one of your nos, so accept it" is the implication.

The cliché offers no comfort. It does nothing for the wounded person except make him clam up about his experience, keeping all the hurt to himself.

In defense of the Christian giving the advice, he wants to help. He feels compelled to defend God, so he repeats what he has heard over and over again. God doesn't need any defense in this situation. He is at work in the prayer's life, and he will help him eventually see the rightness of the no answer.

What we can do is encourage the wounded person to talk about what happened. Encourage him to spill all of his frustration and anger. In this case, a good listener is more important than a good adviser.

When he is finished talking about his experience, gently but firmly encourage him to pray again. Tell him to confess his frustration (and his anger) to God and to reaffirm his trust in God. "God, right now, I don't know why you have responded in this manner. I am angry and hurt, but I'm trying to trust you. I still believe you are a God who answers prayer."

It is very important that we pray right away after receiving God's no answer. It's like driving after an automobile accident. The longer we put off driving after an accident, the harder it is to drive once we do try. The longer we put off praying about our hurt, the harder it becomes. The wound increases as we nurse our frustration. The sooner we pray, the sooner God's healing of our hurt can take place.

Using pat phrases is not an appropriate way to deal with someone's pain. Neither do they adequately describe the way God acts. Some of us, however, lean on simple easy to remember phrases in which to talk. If we must have a simple, easy to remember phrase to describe God's response to our requests, let's just say *God answers.* If we must categorize God, let's categorize him as an answerer.

Notes

1. Herbert Lockyer, *All the Prayers of the Bible* (Grand Rapids: Zondervan Publishing House, 1959), p. 173.
2. Ibid., p. 77.
3. Ibid., p. 162.
4. Ibid., p. 46.

4. Is "Be Careful What You Pray for Because Your Prayers Might Be Answered" Biblically Sound Advice?

"Be careful what you pray for because your prayers might be answered" is a perplexing cliché. It is both true and false, right and wrong.

What's right about the cliché is the "be careful" part. Being careful when we pray is a matter of being prudent. To ask for anything and everything is to look upon prayer as a means of getting, making God a machine that will provide answers. To ask for anything and everything is to disregard who God is. We should never want to ask anything vulgar of a holy God. We should never ask the God who loves all men for anything that would harm another person or show contempt for him. We should never want to ask for things to satisfy our lusts, for we would be asking a righteous God to give us the means for sinning. Being careful about what we pray for serves as a restraint, keeping us aware of God and who he is.

Not only should we be careful about what we ask for, but we should also be careful about the attitude in which we pray. Fervent prayers are sometimes only the passionate cries of selfish hearts—hearts determined to get what they want. Sometimes God will accommodate those selfish hearts when they persist and persist by letting them have their way, but it's not with vindictiveness that he does it. Out of a heart full of love and wisdom, God may let us have our own way in the same way the father of the prodigal son let him leave home. The prodigal's father didn't want to let him go and didn't have to let him go; but in the end he did what was best for his son. So determined was the son that he would not have been able to see the folly of his way without actually experiencing the far country.

The cliché also reminds us that sometimes we expect too much from God's answers. There's sort of an unwritten theology hovering among pray-ers that if we pray for something and God does answer, the answer should be in perfect form. No problems or struggles are to be connected with answers to prayer. If a less-than-perfect answer comes, then we conclude, "I shouldn't have prayed that way. I'll be careful what I ask for next time."

Hezekiah is often accused of praying a prayer that shouldn't have been prayed because of some far-reaching consequences to his answer. Hezekiah prayed to live when Isaiah announced to him that he would die (2 Kings 20:1–3; Isa. 38:1–3; 2 Chron. 32:24). God gave him fifteen additional years of life during which time a son was born to him. Manasseh grew up to become a wicked king in the throne he inherited from his father. His name was synonymous with unrighteousness and bloodshed. The Babylonian captivity and all its woes were laid at the feet of Manasseh. So, the accusers say, if Hezekiah hadn't prayed to live, Manasseh wouldn't have been born, and Judah would not have had to suffer the way she did.

That's laying a great deal on one prayer. God gave Hezekiah fifteen more years of life—life with its struggles, life with its temptations, life with its difficulties, life in which children who have a will of their own can still be born. Hezekiah's sin was not in praying to live but in failing to live the life he was given in an appropriate manner. When Isaiah came to Hezekiah saying that a time was coming when everything in his palace would be carried off to Babylon and some of his descendants would be taken away to serve the king of Babylon, Hezekiah accepted the message. It was not met with the same fervent praying that he met Isaiah's pronouncement of his death. If Hezekiah had cared as much about his descendants as he cared for his own life, things might have gone differently for Manasseh and all of Judah.

An answered prayer about life is not a guarantee that everything that happens in life will be perfect. The life we receive is still life with all its difficulties.

An answered prayer concerning a house does not mean we'll never have any problems with that house. Ownership means responsibility, and things go wrong with houses.

An answered prayer about having a baby does not relieve us from the responsibility of nurturing and raising a child. If the child turns out to be a delinquent at seventeen, we should not look back and say, "God, why did you let me have this child if he were going to turn out like this?"

We might not be so accusatory if we really think about what we are asking for; in that sense, we need to be careful. We need to make certain that our fervent prayers are not selfish cries, demanding our own way. We need to be prudent in our asking, not asking God for anything and everything in recognition of who he is. These are some very fine truths that every pray-er should be aware of; but unfortunately, quoters of the "Be careful what you pray for" cliché usually have something else in mind.

"Be careful what you pray for because your prayers might be answered" generally refers to two specific kinds of experiences. One kind is humorous, and the other is very serious.

The humorous side might go something like this: "I'm the world's most impatient person, so I prayed for patience, and wow! you wouldn't believe all the things that have happened to me. Talk about exercising patience— I've never had to be so patient. Believe me, you'd better be careful (chuckle, chuckle) what you ask for, because God just may give it to you."

The serious side, however, seems to get retold the most, and it's the one we're most concerned about. Although the details change with each person, the story remains basically the same. "My father was at the point of death. I couldn't bear the thought of losing him. How I pleaded with God to let him live. Well, God answered my prayer, all right. He lived five more years as an invalid (or in a vegetable state). Every time I looked at him I thought, *he wouldn't be in this condition if it weren't for me.* Oh, if only I hadn't prayed for him to live." It sounds as though God had wonderful plans for this person until the loved one prayed for him; then zap! God changed his mind and let him really have it.

There are some Old Testament stories that seem to reinforce this kind of interpretation. In Numbers 11:5-33 the Israelite people craved and wanted meat. Weary with their complaining, Moses took their need to the Lord. God answered, "Tell them I'll give them meat; I'll give them meat until they loath it" (v. 20, author's paraphrase). The judge Jephthah wanted victory against the Ammonites. To the Lord he said, "If you will give me victory, I'll give you the first person who comes out to meet me when the battle is over as a burnt offering" (Judg. 11:31, author's paraphrase). Jephthah won the victory, and to our horror the first person to greet him when he returned home was his daughter, his only child. And God answered the request of Israel to have their own king even when having a king meant conscription, forced labor, taxation, and loss of personal liberty.

These Old Testament examples give the impression that we are praying to a mocking God whose gifts may be double-edged, but these examples do not represent the total biblical picture. We are on the redeemed side of God's complete revelation, and that makes all the difference!

What does it mean to live on the redeemed side of God's complete revelation? Very simply, it means we know more. We've progressed in our understanding of God because Jesus came and lived and died and ever lives with us through his Holy Spirit. Until Jesus came, men had never had the opportunity to really and fully know God. They had never seen fully demonstrated the kind of life that God wished them to live.

Jephthah, for example, was a victim of the times in which he lived. The period of the judges is called the dark ages of Israel's history. Their faith was not constant; their standards were low; and their covenant with God was often forgotten. And there were no strong religious leaders on the scene like Moses and Joshua to show them how they were supposed to live. Jephthah was the son of a prostitute; he was forced to leave home; and he went around with a group of worthless men. Consequently, Jephthah may or may not have known that God forbids human sacrifice. *The Broadman Bible Commentary* says that the temptation and practice of human sacrifice punctuated the history of Israel. Only with the passing of time did Israel realize that true Yahweh utterly repudiated such practices. Israel's revelation of God progressed.

If Jephthah had known God as we are privileged to know him through Jesus Christ, he would have known that God doesn't want human sacrifice and that he didn't have to bargain with God for a victory. A bargain was not necessary; all he needed to do was ask.

What bothers us about Jephthah's story is not his lack of knowledge, but God's response to his vow. We can't understand why God would allow Jephthah's only child to be the first one to greet him. The reason we feel this way is because we know Jesus; we cannot see Jesus responding in this way; and this is as it should be. Some scholars have tried to downplay Jephthah's sacrifice to say that she was a spiritual offering and not really burned. We don't know what really happened. To explain the outcome was not the purpose of the compiler of Judges; he only wanted to tell why the custom of Israelite women mourning her death every year was initiated.

Because we don't know what really happened, and because we do know Jesus, we should not use God's answer to Jephthah as a shining example in our prayer lives. Jephthah's experience was a limited one and certainly not to be the norm for Christians. We don't have to bargain with God; Jesus told us to ask that we may receive (John 16:24). Instead of having Moses, the priests, and the prophets to help us with our praying, we have the life and teachings of Jesus, the intercession of Jesus and the Holy Spirit.

Jesus came to show us the Father. When we look at Jesus we see as complete a representation of God, as complete a revelation of the state of God's mind, as our fallible and finite minds are able to comprehend. When we look at Christ, we can get a true idea of God the Father's approachableness in prayer. We can look at what Christ did, how he responded to those who came to him, and what he said.

More than 150 specific cases are recorded in the Gospels of people coming to Jesus asking him for something or about something. He insisted that each case, whether man or devil, must have individual and personal and continual access to him. Nowhere do we see Jesus responding with a spitefulness or hard punch because the person asked or sought him out. He answered patiently with love and understanding. B. H. Carroll said, "What unjust ideas I once had about God! What ideas I have now about God since I studied Jesus! I now know the Father; I know his approachableness." When we have an answer to prayer that appears to indicate that God might be mocking us, we would do well to ask ourselves, *Is this how Jesus would answer?*

Jesus taught men that God is a father who watches over his children with tender care. Matthew recorded Jesus as saying that no earthly father refuses the requests of his son; and God the great Father will never refuse the requests of his children. Jesus used three examples to explain, for Luke 11:11 adds a third to the two Matthew 7:9–10 gives: If a son asks for bread, will his father give him a stone? If a son asks for a fish, will his father give him a serpent? If a son asks for an egg, will his father give him a scorpion?

William Barclay says that the two things cited in each case bear a close resemblance.

The small round limestone stones on the seashore were exactly the shape and color of little loaves. If a son asks for bread, will his father mock him by offering him a stone, which looks like bread but which is impossible to eat?

If a son asks for a fish, will his father give him a serpent? Almost certainly, says Barclay, the serpent is an eel. According to the Jewish food laws, an eel could not be eaten as an article of diet. If a son asks for fish, will his father indeed give him a fish, but a fish that is forbidden for eating and that is useless to eat? Would a father mock his son's hunger like that?

If the son asks for an egg, will his father give him a scorpion? The scorpion is a dangerous little animal. In action it is rather like a small lobster, with claws with which it clutches its victim. Its sting is in its tail, and it brings its tail up over its back to strike its victim. The sting can be exceedingly painful and sometimes even fatal. When the scorpion is at rest its claws and tail are folded in, and there is a pale kind of scorpion, which, when it folds up, would look exactly like an egg. If a son asks for an egg, will his father mock him by handing him a biting scorpion?

With these three examples, Jesus assures us that God does not mock our prayers. God does not respond to our requests with, "OK, I'll give you what you ask for, but you'll be sorry you asked." If we are interpreting an answered prayer in that way, then something is probably wrong with our interpretation and not with God's answer.

Jesus not only showed us what the God to whom we pray is like and taught us about him, but Jesus continues to help us with our praying. The New Testament shows us that Jesus ascended to make intercession for us. Christ is at the right hand of God interceding for us (Rom. 8:34). He lives to make intercession for us (Heb. 7:25), and he appears in the presence of God on our behalf (Heb. 9:24). In Christ we have an advocate in the presence of God (1 John 2:1). Although his act of propitiation was completed once and for all on the cross, his very presence at the right hand of God is an eternal act of intercession on our behalf. While we have no way of fully comprehending what it means to have Jesus as our intercessor, we do know it means this: We do not pray alone.

We are further aided in our asking by the Holy Spirit.

Romans 8:26–27 says, "Likewise the Spirit also helpeth our infirmities: for we know not what we should pray for as we ought: but the Spirit itself maketh intercession for us with groanings which cannot be uttered. And he that searcheth the hearts knoweth what *is* the mind of the Spirit, because he maketh intercession for the saints according to *the will of* God." The Holy Spirit comes to our aid, not by taking over our praying, but by lending a helping hand. He helps us to know what to pray for and helps us make that prayer.

While we know the general objects of prayer and what God's general will is, we may not know what the specific and detailed objects of prayer may be in a given emergency or situation. In our ignorance, it would be easy to pray contrary to God's will. But the Holy Spirit knows not only our minds but also the mind of God and is therefore able to frame our prayers in accordance with God's divine purpose. Whether or not we articulate the request, whether we actually ask for that loved one to live, God still knows the desires of our hearts by the inward working of the Holy Spirit. So it's just not appropriate to berate ourselves for that time in an emergency when we might have asked for a loved one to live. Even if we hadn't asked and had made a more noble plea, God would still have known what it was that we really wanted.

It is with regard to intercessors that the experiences of the children of Israel under Moses and Samuel can help us. When they wanted meat, they asked Moses to call on God. When they wanted a king, they urged Samuel to ask for one. They did not do wrong in bringing their requests to God. Their error consisted in not listening to the response of their spiritual intercessors. Moses gave them God's message of what would happen if they ate meat (Num. 11:24), but they ate it anyway. The people paid no attention to Samuel when he tried to tell them what life under a king would be like (1 Sam. 8:19). They said, "We want one anyway." Often it's not our requests that are wrong but our failure to heed God's reply as spoken to us through Jesus and the Holy Spirit. Our accusation of God's terrible answer may be nothing more than disobedience to the leadership within us.

What an encouragement for us to ask as we consider the full revelation of God as seen in the life of Jesus, in his approachableness, and in his teachings. What reassurance to know that all of our prayers are supported by a double intercession—that of the glorified Christ and of the indwelling Spirit. It's an encouragement and reassurance that it is lacking in the cliché "Be careful what you pray for because your prayers might be answered." Instead, the cliché brings distrust to a relationship based on trust. It makes us vulnerable to the devil's deceptions, and it makes us forget God's intentions for us. And most tragically of all, it keeps us from asking when it is right to do so.

The Christian life is one based on trust. To commit ourselves to Christ is to say, "I believe you are who you say you are, and I am going to live accordingly." Saying "Be careful . . . because your prayers might be answered" plants seeds of doubt in the Christian's mind that the object of his trust can't really be trusted after all. John Claypool explains it in this way. He says that deep in all of us there exists an error, a distortion, a massive misundertanding of the nature of God. We are unwilling to believe that God is good and attentive and concerned about our ultimate welfare; maybe that's why it is easy to believe the cliché.

One Christian magazine showed the picture of a gun with the barrel pointed toward the reader with the caption, "Praying is like looking in the barrel of a loaded gun." What does an illustration like that do to the distortion already within us? It says, "God can't really be trusted." But the Bible says, "We need have no fear of someone who loves us perfectly; his perfect love for us eliminates all dread of what he might do to us. If we are afraid, the reason is fear of what he might do to us and shows that we are not fully convinced that he really loves us" (1 John 4:18, TLB).

Sometimes, we must admit, after we have prayed about something, circumstances begin presenting themselves to make it look as though God might have zapped us. That's exactly what the devil would have us think. He delights in adding fuel to the fire of misunderstanding God, and he's found a good time to do it is right after we've earnestly prayed for something. Here's how the devil disturbed a teenager after she started praying that the farm, which was keeping her parents from attending church, would become less important to them.

Dear Mrs. Poinsett,

I've been praying (like you said) that the farm would be less important to my parents; well, I think it's been answered! Last Sunday my brother (who lives on the farm) and my dad had an argument. Dad ended up walking off, vowing not to come back, ever! I never thought God would break up families just to answer a prayer. I've heard of God working in mysterious ways, but never like this. My whole family has been hurt over it; my mom can't take much more. Dad has been moping around and doesn't say anything. I'm afraid he'll turn to something bad. Like gambling. He used to play poker and games like that until he had the farm to fill his spare time. Would God really break up a family?

Love in Christ,
TINA

If the devil could get Tina to believe that God breaks up families in order to answer prayers, he could stifle her praying for the rest of her life. I hastened to assure her that it is not God's nature to break up families, but it is his nature to answer prayer and she should continue to ask and not quit because of temporary trouble.

Now, Tina's vulnerable spot was after she had prayed but before she received the answer. Sometimes the devil works on us after we've received the answer. When that job we prayed for becomes unbearable. When that baby we've so longed for turns out to be a temperamental, cantankerous child. At those times, it is very important that we not berate ourselves for having asked or God for having answered. That's letting the devil have victory! Instead, we can let the request and God's answer be a comfort to us. "God, I know you can be trusted. I prayed to you, and you gave me what I asked for. You, in your perfect wisdom and love, would not have let me have this (or experience this) if it were not going to be to my benefit and good." Praying this way gives God the channel he needs to supply us with the strength we need to face the situation and to eventually see his good purpose in answering the way he did.

We must remember that when God answers, he is answering with regard to all persons concerned, not just with regard to our request. That paralysis or handicap which came after our request for someone to live may have been for that person's spiritual benefit or for someone else of whom we may not even be aware. We are too prone to see things from our own perspective rather than God's, forgetting that he has purposes and intentions far beyond our understanding. Just because we can't see a purpose in operation doesn't mean there isn't one there.

For many years a woman griped about her only child.

She could never find anything good to say about her daughter, as if she doubted the daughter's love for her. Those who heard her complain were embarrassed to hear her talk, for they sensed that the daughter surely must love her more than the mother indicated. Eventually, the mother suffered a stroke. She was left paralyzed and speechless; but as far as the doctors could tell, her mind was still alert to what was going on around her. Nevertheless, she could not care for herself, so the daughter took her into her home. The daughter kept her mother's room neat; she brought her meals; she bathed and dressed her—all the normal things one would do for a patient in one's home. But the daughter went far beyond that. She manicured her mother's nails. She bought lovely gowns for her to wear, choosing colors that her mother liked and looked nice in. She set her mother's hair, using a rinse on it to enhance the lovely gray. When she could she had fresh flowers on the bedside table. She changed the pictures in the room from time to time so that the mother would not grow weary of looking at the same thing. Everything about the invalid mother's appearance suggested above-average care. She wasn't "just a patient"; she was somebody who was loved.

A casual observer, stopping to call, might wonder why a woman had to lie in bed day after day or why such a gracious person as the daugher had to bear so much responsibility. But if someone who had known the mother earlier in life, someone with a broader perspective, had stopped by, he would be able to see a purpose in it. He would be able to see that she was at last consciously receiving the love she never believed existed. With her attitude the way it was, the mother would never have believed her daughter loved her until she was silently dependent upon her. A broader perspective of the situation identified a purpose that was in all probability hidden from the daughter.

There's a broader perspective in operation behind the answers we receive to our requests—God's perspective. His divine wisdom is in operation. We can trust him to do the right things for us and for those for whom we pray. Not to trust God is to turn the agony of our loved ones into horror stories by saying their suffering would never have happened if we hadn't prayed. When we tell the stories and cap them with "Be careful what you pray for because your prayers might be answered," we contribute to the fear of God already within us; and we keep others from asking when it is right to do so. One conscientious but timid Christian I know has heard this beware-how-you-pray cliché so many times that she is afraid to ask anything specific for her loved ones. Another woman was afraid to pray for her husband to grow spiritually. Her fear was that God would take one of their children to enable her husband to grow! A church refused to meet together to pray for one of their teenagers who was badly injured in an automobile accident for fear God would do something worse to him!

While the cliché does contain some truth, the untruth surrounding it is damaging and harmful. Realizing what God is like through his son Jesus Christ and realizing we pray with the help of Jesus and the Holy Spirit, let's stop quoting the cliché. Instead, let's quote something more appropriate. For a starter, how about Hebrews 4:16? "Let us therefore come boldly unto the throne of grace, that we may obtain mercy, and find grace to help in time of need."

5. Is It Wrong to Beg God to Answer Our Prayers?

If we need biblical examples to support our begging God to grant requests, we have plenty. Some incidents, however, are a matter of interpretation. For instance, one topical Bible lists Paul's thrice-placed request for his thorn in the flesh to be removed as begging. To some of us who have prayed over a period of years for something, three times is barely a beginning.

Here are some of the other prayers listed under *importunity*, a word meaning to beg urgently or to shamelessly persist.

Abraham boldly discussed the plight of the righteous in Sodom with God.

Out of fear of what would happen when he confronted Esau, Jacob wrestled with a representative of God for deliverance.

On behalf of the rebellious, sinful Israelite people, Moses lay face downward in God's presence for forty days and nights, begging him not to destroy them.

In her desperation, Hannah poured out her soul to the Lord for a son.

Ezra, fearful over what would happen to the Jews because of their intermarriages with non-Jews, pleaded for the preservation of the nation and for God's help.

For several days Nehemiah wept and prayed about the conditions in his hometown of Jerusalem. As he prayed, he offered both personal and general confession of sin.

Faced with death, Hezekiah begged the Lord to remember the kind of life he had lived.

Even some of the words used for prayer in the Bible—entreat, petition, implore, beseech—suggest begging.

Standing in stark contrast to these examples is God's nature. It is God's nature to answer prayer; he wants us to open up more and more of ourselves to receive all that he wants to give. His answers are ones we can trust because he is trustworthy. Even his no answers can be trusted. He answers yes much more often than he answers no, and the Bible records few wait answers to specific requests. Even the begging examples we've looked at show his readiness to answer. Abraham's discussion with God over the righteous in Sodom took place in *one* conversation. Jacob's wrestling was for *one* night. Hannah might have prayed earlier in her life for a child, but we do not know if she did. Her weeping and pleading was within *one* prayer. Nehemiah wept *several* days. Paul asked *three* times. Moses, however, prayed forty days and forty nights for the sinful Israelites, and we have no way of knowing how long David might have agonized over his sons. But what do these examples and God's readiness to answer say to those of us who have repeatedly asked for the same thing for *years* instead of days?

Jesus did warn us against vain repetition such as the pagans' prayers. God already knows what we need, he says, so we don't have to keep laying our case before him. Still, sometimes we can't help ourselves, especially when the desire of our hearts is a very tender one or when we want it as much as Hannah wanted a child. Wanting to recognize God's nature and yet wanting so much what we are asking for makes it hard to know when it's all right to keep on asking. Here are some questions we can use to help us decide when continual asking might be appropriate.

1. *Am I asking for the impossible?* When we ask ourselves this question, we are not challenging God's ability to handle the impossible. What we are questioning is our faith to believe the impossible. If we've been asking for something for years and are no closer to it than when we started, maybe we need to consider those faith-sized requests discussed in chapter 2. It could be that we've been asking for the top of the stairs instead of taking one step at a time, and we've asked so long that our request has become a vain repetition. We need to break the request down to the first step, a portion our faith can handle, and pray about that instead of continuing to tackle the impossible.

2. *Do I really want the answer?* That may seem like a peculiar question to ask about something we've been asking for so long, but Jesus asked a similar question to a man who had been sick for thirty-eight years. Jesus asked him if he wanted to get well (John 5:5–6). Why wouldn't anyone who had been sick for that long want to be healed? But the truth is that there are some people who are sick who don't want to get well. To be well, they would have to take up life with all of its responsibilities again. Those who serve them would go back to their regular lives and perhaps leave them lonely. Those who bestow attention on them might turn their affections to someone else. It is sometimes more comfortable to be sick and to endure pain than to face the harshness and realities of life. That very prayer we've been praying may remain unanswered because we don't want it answered. We wouldn't want the responsibility that goes with the answer.

3. *What does my continual asking indicate about my concept of self?* Many of the biblical prayers of importunity are pleas for forgiveness of sin. These prayers are found in the Old Testament where men were under the sacrificial system, where they did not have access to grace as we do. Although they were looking forward to the coming of Christ, they had no way of grasping all that would mean. On the redeemed side of God's complete revelation, we know the sacrifice for sin has been paid once and for all. Our past sins, the sins we are now committing, and the sins we will commit are all forgiven, but do we pray as though they have *all* been forgiven?

Interestingly enough, there will occur some few sins in our lives for which we will not feel forgiven. We confess and plead for forgiveness over and over, waiting for God's forgiveness, which we already have (1 John 1:9). What we probably have not done is forgive ourselves. By pleading over and over, we are really saying, *I can't forgive myself. I cannot accept what I have done.* Instead of persisting in a prayer for forgiveness, it might be wiser if we changed our prayer to, "God, help me accept myself as the sinner I am. Help me admit what I've done wrong."

4. *What does my continual asking indicate about my concept of God?* Do we look at God as the neighbor who begrudgingly gave the bread or as the unjust judge described by Jesus in two of his parables (Luke 11:5-8; 18:1-8)? Both the neighbor and the judge had to be worn down by persistent pleading.

For many of us the neighbor in the other house and the unjust judge personify the way we tend to think of God. But we must remember that Jesus often used contrast as well as similarity in his teaching. And in these two stories Jesus was teaching the antithesis rather than the likeness of God.

The neighbor next door and the unjust judge correspond perfectly with how pagan religions regarded deity. Pagan gods were indifferent. The glory of being a god in pagan thoughts was not having to worry about earth or the people here. Thus, the image of one who was asleep and utterly unconcerned about the problem of no food for an unexpected guest, or a judge who was unjust in the first place with no compassion for the widow, corresponds exactly with how paganism understood the attitude of heaven.

If this is our view of God, it logically follows that prayer should take the form of persistent begging. After all, given the indifference of his neighbor, the man who needed food did the only thing he could do in the night—wear down his resistance until he gave him what he needed. Likewise, the widow had to wear down the judge. One way to cope with reluctance is to keep badgering.

When we repeat the same request over and over again, are we saying that God is reluctant to give? Do we think, *If I keep up long enough God will have to answer?* Are we saying that God is not good, not attentive, and not concerned about our ultimate welfare?

5. *Is my faith in God or in my persistence?* These questions we're using to examine our continual asking are not meant to imply that it is always wrong. As Jesus was teaching in these two parables of the sound-asleep neighbor and the unjust judge, persistence in prayer is important.

Persistence guarantees the sincerity of our desire. Our asking again and again shows that we are serious in our request; it wasn't just a passing idea.

Through persistent praying, our wills are molded toward receiving what we are asking for. We may have the desire before we are ready to receive, so persistent praying helps us prepare.

Persistent praying can be a tool in our spiritual warfare. With the devil continuously working trying to erode our faith, we need the exercise of bringing the petition daily before the Lord. After we pray for something, the devil will work on us, trying to wear down our confidence in the Lord. Our bringing it back to the Lord says to the devil, "You lose!"

Persistence can be a beautiful act of faith. R. A. Torrey says that God delights in holy boldness that will not take no for an answer. Like the Syrophoenician woman (Mark 7:26), we can persist in our asking as she did until God can say of us as Jesus said to her, "Great is thy faith." Faith needs to find some resistance before it can be called out in any strength.

Persistent praying is important, but a word of caution is needed. The belief in the importance of persistent praying can tempt us to believe that if we ask enough times, God will have to answer. This is putting our faith and confidence in *our* ability to persist and not in the God who answers prayer. It is right to persist in asking when it is an act of faith in what God can do; but when we make it an act of faith in what we can do, persistence is wrong.

6. *Has there been any change in the situation since I started praying about it?* Have I received any "light" on the situation that shows me God is at work? Any change, any evidence that God is working should be an encouragement to continue to persist. The situation may be a complicated one, involving more wills than our own. New light on the situation is God's encouragement: "Pray on; your persistence is important in this matter. The full answer will come."

But what if there has been no change, nothing to indicate a recognizable response on God's part? Then it's time we started examining the request. Once, when I had been asking for three things in particular, God immediately granted two of them. I continued to pray for the third and soon became frustrated in asking so many times when God had so graciously and quickly granted the other two. A little conversation with myself helped.

"Brenda, you believe God answers prayer, don't you?"

"Yes, I believe God answers prayer."

"Why is it he granted only two things and not the third when it is his nature to answer prayer?"

"I don't know."

"Could there be a difference in the requests?"

"I don't think . . . wait a minute, I believe you've got something there."

My third request was different than the other two. The two answers I immediately received concerned things. But the third item was a situation I thought beyond my ability to handle. If God would handle it I wouldn't have to; yet it was a situation that I would have to repeat several times in life. I needed to learn how to handle it, so I changed my request. "God, give me the wisdom and insight I need to handle this situation." And like the answerer I knew him to be, God quickly responded and helped me work through the situation.

7. What I was really wanting was an escape, which gives us another question to consider, *Is my prayer a request for an escape?* If God had answered my request exactly as I prayed, would I escape a situation about which I now have no courage? Sometimes when life gets frustrating for my seven-year-old, he says, "Why doesn't Jesus give us the power to turn into Captain Marvel?" Some

of us pray with the same longing, asking God to give us supernatural ability to rise above life's difficulties, when facing them head-on would, in the long run, do more for our spiritual growth.

We're not saying that it is wrong to pray for an escape. But if we've been praying for an escape for a long time and God hasn't answered, then perhaps he is saying to us that we need to learn to endure. What God may be saying in response to our often-repeated plea is "Forget the escape. It's time to act courageously. We'll forge through this thing together."

8. *What would happen if I stopped praying? The Living Bible* humorously records the Lord as saying to Moses, "Quit praying and get the people moving! Forward, march!" (Ex. 14:15). As the Israelites bemoaned their condition before a sea without a bridge, Moses had the solution in hand. There was no need for prayer. The Lord's next words were, "Use your rod" (v. 16). In other words, *I've already answered your prayer. I've already given you the means to handle this situation. Now get with it.*

Joshua 7 records a similar response from God, although the circumstances are very different. The Israelites attacked Ai and lost. In fear of what would happen if their enemies knew they had been defeated, they threw themselves on the ground and wailed before the Lord. "Lord, what are you going to do about this? What are you going to do to protect your honor?"

But the problem wasn't with the Lord. "The Lord said to Joshua, 'Get up! Why are you lying on the ground like this?' " (Josh. 7:10, TEV). Israel had sinned. God had told them not to take from Jericho anything that was to be destroyed, and they disobeyed. They needed to purify themselves, not to pray. And sure enough, when the purification was done Israel had the power to capture Ai.

Now, this may be the first book you have read on prayer which suggests that you quit praying; but that is exactly what some of us need to do about some requests we've been repeating and repeating. Perhaps God has already given us our "rod" to handle the situation. And instead of using it, we've prayed on and on as if God had never heard. Perhaps we've refused to acknowledge a sin in our life that keeps us from having victory. There could be other reasons, and it won't hurt to stop praying for a while and examine the situation. To our surprise, we may discover that God has already answered.

9. *How would I act if I knew for a certainty that God was going to answer my request?* The great intercessor Rees Howells believed that once he prayed an item through, it was a sin if he continued to ask for it. To him continual asking was the same as doubting. Sometimes the praying through took several days or longer; but once Howells was assured of God's answer, he never asked again. Even without the visible evidence of an answer, Howells went on his way in full confidence that the answer would come. He asked and acted in faith.

Begging is a negative action that will affect us when we continually petition the Lord. ("Oh, Lord, how many times must I bring this request before you?") How much better it would be for us to ask and act in faith. Some of us, who are not yet in Rees Howells' league, may find that hard to do. We can, however, express our request in a more positive manner. After we have prayed several times about a request, laying it before the Lord until we feel that we have sufficiently presented our case, we can alter our request: "Father, I believe you are going to grant my request (name it). Today, I'm going to show you I believe you will by not worrying about it (or by some other act—perhaps an act of preparation for what we are going to receive)." In this way even our actions can become prayers.

The psalmist encouraged us to pour out our hearts before the Lord who is our refuge (Ps. 62:8). As long as our hearts are deeply touched by the cares of this life, there will be times when we cannot help but beg our case before the Lord. At the same time, however, we must keep in mind that it is God's nature to answer and to answer quickly when he can.

Considering our nature, begging is understandable.

Considering God's nature, there's a better way to ask. And that way is to ask and act in faith.

6. Should We Have Prayer Lists? How Long Should We Keep Someone or Something on the List?

In answering our previous chapter questions, we have looked to the Bible for our answers. We can hardly do that with this question. Although Paul often speaks of "making mention of you in my prayers," we could hardly refer to that as a biblical basis for having prayer lists. Writing down prayer requests is an option for the pray-er. He may choose to do it, or he may ignore it and still have a meaningful prayer life.

Some pray-ers depend upon a list for the simple reason that they can't remember everything they want to pray for. For this kind of pray-er, it amounts to about the same thing as keeping a grocery list. It's an aid to memory and nothing more. When prayer time comes, they have a number of things before them, ready to be prayed for.

Others like the benefit that comes from writing down the requests. In this case, the list is usually not made ahead of time as it is with the memory-jogger. The list is made as the pray-er prays. He uses it to nail down the fact of his praying. When my mind is a jumble and I find being coherent difficult, I write down my requests as I pray. I'll speak the request out loud and then I write it down as if to say, "There, I've prayed about it. I've asked, and now God is going to answer." When a list is used in this way, it becomes a faith-builder.

A prayer list can also help us be specific in our asking,

in our praising, and in our confessing. When we write our requests down on paper we get a clearer idea of what it is we are asking for. We can see if we are really asking for anything specific. We can see if our request is too broad and if it needs to be whittled down to a size our faith can handle.

Some pray-ers keep notebooks, jotting down on the left-hand page a request and the date. On the right-hand page, space is reserved for recording the date of the answer. One pray-er records all his requests in black. When he receives the answer, he writes a big red "praise the Lord" over the request. Then his list of specific requests becomes his list of specific praises.

One person who writes out his requests and numbers them 1, 2, 3, etc. says, "Often I make confessions of sin in the same way. As honestly and as fairly as I can, I wait before God until he lays on my heart things that grieve him. Then I write them out plainly on a piece of paper. I keep that before me for a few days until I feel I have gotten the victory, and God knows and I know that I have honestly judged those sins and have tried to put them away. But you may be sure that I do not leave that list of confessed sins around where anybody else can see it!"

As the lists are kept and prayed over, it's a thrilling experience to see the requests answered. But the lists have a way of growing, sometimes faster than the answers come. In our excitement at "seeing" the answers on paper we begin adding more items, not thinking ahead to the amount of praying that may be involoved.

In one church in which I was a member, we were encouraged to pray for the missionaries listed on the denominational calendar of prayer. The state convention also put out a prayer list. Likewise, the association put out one; and the church, too, published a weekly prayer list. In addition, the Sunday School department I was in kept a running list. (We ran over each item every Sunday morning trying to decide if it should stay on the list for another week!) Now, anyone who can effectively pray for all the people and all the items on all those lists is quite a pray-er. Most of us can't; and unless we are careful, our lists can become overwhelming. When that happens, praying becomes a burden and loses its vitality.

As the lists grow, prayer becomes a record-keeping job: writing down each request, keeping track of the list, recording the answers. One conscientious pray-er's list has grown so long that she keeps two—list A and list B to use on alternate days. One writer suggests lists for each day of the week: intercession for non-Christians on Monday, thanksgiving and praise on Tuesday, confession of sins on Wednesday, etc. Unless we are careful, this kind of record-keeping praying can rob our prayers of spontaneity which is so vital to making prayer a real conversation. It can also rob us of time. As one pray-er said, "I had great lists but little time to pray."

A built-in problem with prayer lists is knowing when to take someone off. No one likes to think that prayer for him has stopped, and conscientious pray-ers are hesitant to remove a name, thinking, *If I prayed a little harder or a little more fervently, maybe this request could still be answered.* With most of our personal requests, we will soon have a recognizable answer. But many of those things added to our list are intercessions for others whose wills we may not have complete knowledge of. Distance or incomplete communication may separate us, and we pray on and on, waiting for a recordable result. Possibly the burden of the request lifts, but still there's a hesitancy to remove a request without an answer when it's written in black and white.

A written request sometimes locks us in to expecting a certain kind of answer. Looking at a request over and over again may set our minds to expecting God to answer in just the way we have asked. Like Moses and Joshua, we may pray right on past the real answer.

Lists can help us in our asking—helping us remember what we want to ask, improving our faith by nailing down requests, and aiding us in being specific. But lists can also rob our prayers of their vitality. Lists require record keeping, make us feel guilty, and lock in our expectations. How can we deal with prayer requests and improve our asking without sacrificing vitality?

We can start by not keeping the lists. We can throw the lists away after we've used them as memory-joggers or faith-builders. Not hanging on to them eliminates the need for record keeping. In this way, lists help us with our asking but do not become burdensome or rob us of meaningful prayer conversation.

Throwing away the lists eliminates the record-keeping, burdensome part of praying; but it also eliminates the joy of seeing a written record of answers to our prayers. I found that a prayer journal gives me the benefits of the writing of requests and the answers without sacrificing meaningful prayer conversation. In a spiral notebook, I record requests that are especially significant to me. I do not try to include all the things I am going to pray for; neither do I feel that by writing down the request, I am committed to see the request through. Writing down is my act of faith-building. The next time I pray I start a new page, not looking back to what I have previously written. Not looking back eliminates the feeling that I have to keep going over and over each item. Still, the record is there. And every once in a while, *for the joy of it*, I flip back through the pages and note God's answers. If I need a memory-jogger, the requests are there for that, too.

Incidentally, seeing our prayers over a period of time can be quite revealing. I was surprised at how morbid mine were. The evidence stood out when I examined my prayers in light of God's answers and saw how all along he had been working.

Throwing away the lists and keeping a prayer journal are two ways we can get the best from writing down requests without getting caught in the pitfalls. Maybe the pitfalls wouldn't be so much of a problem if we could better handle the requests that come our way. We need to do more praying on the spot instead of promising to pray later. When a request comes to our attention, we can stop whatever we are doing and pray for the situation then and there. We may not be in a position to close our eyes or kneel, but we can mentally push out everything else and pray aloud, asking the other person to join us. If the request comes in a letter we're answering, we can stop writing and pray and tell the person that we have done so, maybe including the very words that we've prayed. If the request comes to us over the phone, we can say, "Let's pray about it right now." The real benefit here is that the other person hears our prayers. He hears us ask in faith and is helped by the confidence we express in God's willingness to answer.

Unfortunately, some Christians are not thinking of the time and effort that must go into fervent praying when they make requests. In that department where we ran over the list each Sunday morning, one lady raised her hand and said, "I wish you would remember my grandparents in Texas."

"Fine," said the superintendent, "what are their names so I can add them to our list?"

"Uh . . . I don't know," she replied, "I've always just called them Grandma and Grandpa."

If she wasn't concerned enough about her grandparents to know their names, how could a roomful of adults seriously consider praying for them? That was a request she could and should handle alone. (Let's hope she begins by learning their names!)

Sometimes a need is so overwhelming that we cannot pray for it alone. Sometimes the power of the devil is so strong that Christians must band together to fight against it. Sometimes we are too upset to pray and must ask someone else to pray for us. But there are also many requests that we can pray for and receive without the aid of other Christians. Heaven does not have to be bombarded for God to hear us.

When people ask us to pray with them, we can discern their sincerity by praying on the spot with them. Their willingness or unwillingness to pray is a good indicator of the seriousness of their request. How they pray will reveal their will in the matter, what they will allow God to do in their situation. That will help us know how to pray for them. Instead of asking for all requests, maybe the department superintendent should have said, "What prayer requests do you have today that you would like us to pray with you about right now?" Or maybe a gentler approach would be, "What requests do you have that you cannot pray through alone and that you specifically need our help with?"

By praying on the spot, we pray, yes; but we do not promise further involvement. Does this mean we won't pray for the request again? Not necessarily. We should continue to pray for the request as often as the Holy

Spirit brings it to mind. Then we are praying at his leadership and not because we promised. This eliminates the problem of trying to depend upon our own memory and of creating long lists.

Rees Howell gave his life to the task of praying for others, and he achieved remarkable results. He did not believe he should intercede in depth for every situation that came to his attention; he prayed only for those needs given to him by the Holy Spirit.

To pray in the leadership of the Holy Spirit is not an escape from responsibility; we are not necessarily going to pray less following his leadership rather than our written prayer lists; but we will be praying for those things in which our intercession is important. Our prayers are going to make a difference when we respond to his leadership to perform a work of grace in someone's life. They are Christ's prayers being offered through us. Knowing that should bring some vitality to our praying!

Praying at the Holy Spirit's prompting adds to the importance of having a set time and place to pray. We need quiet moments in which we hear the voice of the Spirit. Rees Howell was a busy man when he first learned the secret of praying only at the Spirit's prompting. He was a miner, working from seven in the morning until four-thirty in the afternoon. He went every evening to a nearby village, five nights a week for meetings at a mission he worked in and two nights for visiting. His biographer says the only time Howell had to pray was on that two-mile walk each evening to the village, one mile of which was over a lonely common. Howell always tried to be alone for that mile and walked in the attitude of prayer so he could receive the message of the Holy Spirit and pray accordingly.

Maybe this is the kind of praying Paul had in mind

when he mentioned "Praying always with all prayer and supplication in the Spirit" (Eph. 6:18). Certainly, it's a kind of praying that is superior to long, much-repeated prayer lists. That is not to say that the writing down of requests cannot be an aid to our asking, but no list will ever do for our asking what praying Holy-Spirit-inspired prayers will do. At those times we can ask with a certainty, knowing that we are indeed praying in accordance with God's will.

7. When Is It Right to Put Out the "Fleece"?

Putting out the fleece is a special kind of asking prayer. The phrase comes from the Old Testament story of Gideon when he sought proof that God was going to use him to rescue the Israelites. The story in Judges 6 tells how the Israelites had been suffering heavily under Midianite rule. They cried to the Lord for deliverance. God responded with plans to deliver them under the leadership of Gideon. Gideon, however, wasn't so sure about God's plan of deliverance. The idea of his being Israel's leader was so preposterous that he sought tangible confirmation.

Gideon put a piece of wool (the fleece) on the threshing room floor and asked God to keep the ground around it dry and let the dew gather only on the fleece. That would be his sign to know that God was going to use him to deliver Israel.

When God honored his request, Gideon was still not convinced. He asked again, this time for the more miraculous process of leaving the fleece dry and the ground around it wet. Again God honored his request, confirming indeed that Gideon was his choice for leadership.

Christians have so identified with Gideon's story that when they pray similarly, laying out a prescribed condition to confirm God's will, they call it putting out the fleece. While pieces of wool are no longer used, Christians do pray conditionally. They prescribe signs they will recognize, signs as tangible for them as Gideon's fleece was for him.

"Lord, if it is your will that I enter the preaching ministry, I pray that my church will ask me to speak on layman's Sunday."

"Father, if it be your will for me to go to college, I pray for a source of help. You know I do not have the money to go, but I will enroll and make plans to attend, if you will give me one source of help outside my own efforts to let me know of your desire."

"Dear God, you know how miserable and dissatisfied I am in my job. I can stay with it if I am really certain that it is your will. The trouble is that I am no longer certain. If it is your desire for me to leave, I pray that another job will be offered to me."

Gideon's story is not the only one of its kind in the Bible. Hezekiah asked for a sign of assurance that God was going to heal him and let him live. Abraham's conscientious servant put out a sign to clarify God's choice for the bride of Isaac, and the Bible records a lot of if-then prayers. But there must be something about Gideon's experience that especially intrigues us. What is there about Gideon's experience that attracts us? Was it the fraility of Gideon's faith? Was it the preposterousness of what God was asking him to do? Was it the time in which he lived? Let's answer these questions to find out why Gideon's experience is a meaningful one for Christians.

Although Gideon eventually is listed among the heroes of the faith (Heb. 11:32) for winning a victory over the Midianites with just three hundred men, he was not a man of great faith at the time of the fleece. Prior to the fleece, Gideon had encountered an angel of the Lord who told him he would rescue Israel. Gideon had to have proof that the angel was the Lord's messenger. In addition to honoring the terms of the proof, God gave Gideon his word that he would be with him (Judg. 6:16). God protected his life after he followed God's instructions to tear down his father's altar to Baal and the symbol of Asherah. The tribes also agreed to follow Gideon's leadership (Judg. 6:33-35). An angel, God's word, preservation of life, willing followers—pretty good signs of God's leadership and call—but they were not enough for Gideon. He asked for more, and God graciously accommodated himself to Gideon's request.

As a case study, we can look at Gideon's experience and say that his response to God was not a very valorous one. But as honest Christians, we must admit that there are times when our faith sinks to such a low ebb that valor becomes the least of our concerns. At those times it seems we can do no more than Gideon did and lay a condition before the Lord: "God, if you are real, then show me yourself all over again."

Perhaps Gideon's self-image had something to do with his frail faith. Gideon said, "But Lord, how can I rescue Israel? My clan is the weakest in the tribe of Manasseh, and I am the least important member in my family" (Judg. 6:15, TEV). Gideon did not see himself as a hero, but God did. "The Lord answered, 'You can do it because I will help you. You will crush the Midianites as easily as if they were only one man'" (Judg. 6:16, TEV).

Saul made a response similar to Gideon's when Samuel indicated to him that he would be Israel's leader. "I belong to the tribe of Benjamin, the smallest tribe in Israel, and my family is the least important one in the tribe. Why, then, do you talk like this to me?" (1 Sam. 9:21, TEV). God was just as gracious to Saul as he was to Gideon and gave him proof of his calling (1 Sam. 10:1).

Moses gave excuses. So did Jeremiah. God gave Moses the rod to prove his leadership to the Israelites (Ex. 4: 2–5). Because of Jeremiah's timidity, he gave him words to speak and visions of God's promise of protection.

Apparently, from what we can gather from these men, we have a hard time seeing ourselves as God sees us. We are so aware of our own inabilities and weaknesses that we lock ourselves in by them and lose our perspective of what can be done with God's help. So when God does call, we respond, "Me? You mean you want me?" And if the idea is as preposterous to us as it was to Gideon, we, too, may be tempted to seek confirmation. "God, if you want me, then . . ."

Further understanding can be gained about Gideon's reaction to God's call when we examine the time in which he lived. Gideon lived in the dark ages of Israel's history. The Israelites were no longer held together by the strong leadership of men like Moses and Joshua. Their commitment to the covenant was weak. To them Yahweh was the God of history, not the God of the present. They remembered him as the one who led them out of Egypt and eventually to the land they now occupied. They looked around at their neighbors, whom they were supposed to have driven out, and saw that they believed their gods controlled the rains, springs, and vegetation. So the Israelites thought it was to their advantage to worship them as well. Consequently, they fell into the hands of the Midianites.

The Midianites terrorized them. The Bible says that they were as thick as locusts and that their camels were too many to count (Judg. 6:5–6). With an enemy like that and with a God who Gideon thought had abandoned them, Gideon was scared. His reaction was not that of a man rich in a personal relationship with God, but that of a man who had never seen for himself God at work. When we know that about him, his questioning the angel's validity and his conditional praying seem more understandable. And because God needed a man to deliver his people, he honored Gideon's unusual requests.

Seeing Gideon in light of his background may help us understand why God might honor some fleeces that aren't becoming to his nature. Some of us have used the color of a car, the ringing of the phone, or robins on a fence as prescribed conditions in our prayers to determine God's will. God honored those fleeces, not because they were appropriate but because they were the best we had to offer at the time. There are things that are allowable in a child that are not allowable in an adult. The child does not know any better. Even though Christians live on the redeemed side of God's revelation, all Christians are not aware of what that means. A new Christian or a Christian who has not grown may not be aware of all that is at his disposal to help him determine God's will. Out of his lack of knowledge, he offers a prayer that would not be appropriate for a more mature Christian; and God responds and honors the prescribed condition. The pray-er's fleece, as feeble as it is, says, *I believe you are who you say you are, and I believe you will respond* (Heb. 11:6).

God knoweth our frame (Ps. 103:14); and because he does, he is gracious to us when our faith is frail, when our self-image is poor, and when our knowledge is lacking. We should not, however, take advantage of God's grace and make fleeces a consistent way of asking in our prayers. To do so would be to ignore the nature of the Christian life.

Christians possess the Word of God. We have it in hand.

While God does allow for our lack of knowledge at times, that is no excuse for not studying the Bible and finding in it the guidance we need for our lives. The guidelines are there; and where the Bible specifically points out something for us as God's will, it would be wrong for us to put out a fleece about it. That is not an appropriate prayer for a Christian. Confession and restitution are important biblical principles. When the Bible clearly speaks about a matter, putting out a fleece about it is wrong.

If the Bible does not speak specifically about the situation, then a Christian should take what he does know of God's guidelines and apply it as specifically as he can under the leadership of the Holy Spirit. For example, a Christian needs help in deciding about a job. The Bible speaks to him about all of his life, including his work, being committed to God. It gives him some guidelines on kinds of work that would not be appropriate for a Christian to do; but when those conditions are met, he may still be uncertain about taking a specific job. This is when he needs to listen to the voice of the Holy Spirit. Inwardly, the Holy Spirit will let us know what God would have us do. Some Christians describe it as "a sense of peace"; others say "a feeling of rightness" or "I just couldn't see doing anything else." In some way, in a way we can recognize, the Holy Spirit will direct us.

Another source to *accompany* the Bible and the Holy Spirit to confirm God's will is the advice of mature Christians. There are times when we get so distraught at our situation that we cannot see the Bible clearly or hear the voice of the Holy Spirit. That's when another Christian not caught up in the emotion of the situation can help us. He can see the situation clearly; he knows us; and, most of all, he knows the Bible and the Holy Spirit.

There's a wealth of guidance available to us from older-in-the-Lord-than-we-are Christians, and it is most appropriate to seek their help.

Before a growing Christian puts out a fleece, he should ask himself, *What is there about this situation that compels me to put out the fleece? Why can I not determine God's will through the Bible, the inward witness of the Holy Spirit, or the counsel of Christian friends?* These questions would help us restrain ourselves regarding fleeces, for restraint is necessary. There's a subtle temptation involved with fleeces. Once we've experienced a few, we want more. They are thrilling, tangible proofs of God's existence. They are clear—no doubt about which way God wants us to go once a fleece has been honored. Because they are so thrilling and clear, the temptation is to make all of our decisions in the same way, ignoring the fact that the Christian is to walk by faith. Continual use of fleeces is to make prayer a process of divination. Heads, we go. Tails, we stay.

Maybe this is what happened to Gideon. So many signs were given him—so many exciting things were done—that when the battle was over and they were free of Midianites, Gideon developed an ephod. We are not exactly sure what an ephod was, but we do know it was a device used to find out God's will. We don't have ephods any more. We don't have Urim and Thummim as were used by the priests. Neither do we cast lots as men of old did to determine God's will. We have the Bible; we have the Holy Spirit; we have our fellow Christians. We walk by faith, not by tangible signs.

As great a life as Gideon had in leading the Israelites to victory, he also led them into sin. The ephod that he built became an idol to them. They worshiped the ephod instead of the God who delivered them. All the miracles and signs granted in the life of Gideon did not guarantee appropriate followship. When the crisis was past, he led them astray.

Peter put a condition before Jesus: "Lord, if it is really you, order me to come out on the water to you." "Come!" answered Jesus, and Peter got out of the boat and started walking. But did he continue? Peter had his condition satisfied, but it was not enough to sustain him on the water (Matt. 14:28-29, TEV).

As clear and exciting as fleeces may be, as helpful as they are when our faith is frail, our self-image is suffering, or our knowledge is lacking, they are not the substance on which we are to base our lives. Jesus said, "If a man love me, he will keep my words: and my Father will love him, and we will come unto him, and make our abode with him" (John 14:23). It is to the man who keeps his commandments that God reveals himself. The children of Israel would never have needed Gideon and the fleece if they had been living as they were supposed to live. If their neighbors had been driven out as they were supposed to have been, the Israelites wouldn't have been oppressed by them. Commitment is what is important, and there is no substitute for that.

8. Is It Wrong to Pray to Jesus or to the Holy Spirit?

As we approach this question, I am reminded of something a college sociology professor said to us as we began a course in race relations. An experienced teacher of many years, he said, "If you are prejudiced now, you will be even more prejudiced when you finish this course. If you are not prejudiced now, you will be even less prejudiced when you have finished." His statement startled me, but as the term progressed I saw that he was right. A whole course full of enlightened information is not enough to change the set mind.

That's the way it is with the question of to whom we pray. There are two sides to the answer, and each side seems pretty adamant about their position. Therefore, it would be easy to approach this question by looking for information to bolster our position. But for the sake of improving our praying, let's try to be open-minded, for both sides have some good things to say.

One side, which teaches that we should pray to the Father only, says it is wrong to pray to the Holy Spirit or to Jesus. The basis for their belief is a simple one, easily verified by Scriptures.

First and foremost, this side says that Jesus prayed to the Father. "Father, if thou be willing" (Luke 22:42), "Father, forgive them" (Luke 23:34), "Father, into thy hands" (Luke 23:46), "Father, save me from this hour"

(John 12–27), and "Father, glorify thy name" (John 12:28). In his high priestly prayer of John 17, Jesus addressed God as Father, Holy Father, O Father, and O righteous Father. If Jesus prayed to the Father, that's who we should pray to.

Not only did Jesus pray to the Father, but the scriptural pattern of prayer taught by Jesus addresses the Father.

"But thou, when thou prayest, enter into thy closet, and when thou hast shut thy door, pray to thy Father which is in secret; and thy Father which seeth in secret shall reward thee openly" (Matt. 6:6).

"After this manner therefore pray ye: Our Father which art in heaven, Hallowed be thy name" (Matt. 6:9).

"And he said unto them, When ye pray, say, Our Father which art in heaven, Hallowed be thy name" (Luke 11:2).

Jesus further taught that prayers should be made in his name. In his last teachings to his disciples as recorded by John, Jesus encouraged them to ask in his name. Twice he said, "Whatsoever ye shall ask the Father in my name" (John 15:16 and John 16:23). Therefore, this side reasons, if we are to ask in Jesus' name, it would be inappropriate to address our prayers to him.

This side does acknowledge the roles of Jesus and the Holy Spirit in praying, but does so without specifically addressing them. They say we address the Father in the name of the Lord Jesus Christ through the ministry of the Holy Spirit. One person expressed his viewpoint in this way: "Our prayers are validated by Jesus Christ and are interpreted to God the Father by the Holy Spirit." The Holy Spirit helps in preparing our case, and Jesus helps in presenting our case; so it would not be appropriate to address our requests to them.

The other side, which is not as easily verified by the Scriptures, says that it is not only right but is also highly desirable to pray to Jesus and to the Holy Spirit as well as to the Father. This side does not deny or contradict any of the arguments of the first side, but they do say the guiding principle in those verses might not necessarily be that we are to address our prayers only to the Father.

It was only natural that Jesus would pray to the Father. In fact, he was the one who let us know that it was right to call God *Father*. In the time of Jesus, the name of God was so sacred that ordinary people were not supposed to speak it. The sacred name was never pronounced except by the high priest when he went into the holy of holies on the Day of Atonement. Jesus came and showed us that God is accessible and that we can all speak to him. As the obedient son, Jesus called God Father and showed us God's true nature. When Jesus called God *Father*, he let us know that we could come to God with the simple trust and confidence with which a little child comes to a father whom he knows and loves and trusts. Jesus' calling God *Father* does not imply that it is wrong for us to address him or the Holy Spirit in prayer. What other way would have been appropriate for Jesus to pray?

The scriptural pattern of prayer is what we call the Lord's Prayer. To say that the Lord's Prayer teaches that we are to address only the Father is to say we can only pray for what is in the Lord's Prayer and in that order. Jesus' concern in his teachings of Matthew 6:6,9 and Luke 11:2 is not to teach the disciples who to pray to. They knew who to pray to. His concern was to teach them how to pray and how to avoid praying like hypocrites and pagans.

The teaching of Jesus to pray in his name doesn't rule out praying to him. Although Jesus said, "Whatsoever ye shall ask the Father in my name," he also said, "If you ask me for anything in my name, I will do it" (John 14:14, TEV) on the same occasion. Not all of the versions we read have *me* inserted, but it is in the oldest manuscripts. Wasn't Jesus contradicting himself? No; what he is really saying is, "If you ask the Father, he will give it—if you ask me . . . I will do it." It's the same thing.

But what about those other words of Jesus spoken on the same occasion: "In that day ye shall ask me nothing" (John 16:23)? B. H. Carroll says there's no contradiction in the Greek. *Asking* in John 14:14 means to pray. *Asking* in John 16:23 means to ask a question. Jesus, just after answering a masked question of the disciples, was reminding them of a time near at hand when they could ask him no questions. He would be away, and they would have to consult the Holy Spirit, who would be their teacher.

This argument may seem a bit detailed; but to those who pray to Jesus and to the Holy Spirit, it is meaningful. In light of the early manuscripts, they see no impropriety in speaking to Jesus or to the Holy Spirit. In the next chapter, when we examine what praying in Jesus' name means, we'll be able to see that that would not disallow praying to Jesus.

Neither does this side deny the functions of the three persons of the Trinity in prayer. In fact, they say, addressing the three persons in recognition of their functions enhances prayer and makes it a more meaningful experience.

"Jesus, I thank you that you not only interceded for me once on the cross, but that you continue to intercede on my behalf. As I struggle with the cares of this world and fail so often, I am comforted to know that you are at God's right hand, pleading my case. I thank you, Jesus, that I do not pray alone."

"O Holy Spirit, this situation is beyond my comprehension and understanding. I simply do not know how to pray for it. I cannot even see my own will in it, let alone God's. But because of the seriousness of the situation, I feel compelled to pray. Holy Spirit, help me prepare my case. Help me pray this through."

So the second side doesn't really contradict the first side. They would just like to add to it. The second side says we pray to God. Sometimes we pray to God the Father, sometimes to God the Son, and sometimes to God the Spirit. In some way we do not understand, they are all God—coequal, coessential, and coeternal. To say it is wrong to pray to Jesus or the Holy Spirit is to say that they are less than God.

The early church recognized Jesus as God. In the Septuagint, the oldest Greek version of the Old Testament, *kurios* (the Greek word for Lord) is the word regularly used to translate the name of God, Yahweh, or Jehovah. After his resurrection, Jesus became known as *kurios*. Paul preached "Jesus Christ the Lord" (2 Cor. 4:5). [There is] One Lord, one faith, one baptism (Eph. 4:5). The confession that Jesus Christ is Lord and the belief in the resurrection are necessary elements in salvation (Rom. 10:9). The Christian in his heart must sanctify Christ as Lord (1 Pet. 3:15). Paul believed that a day would come when every tongue would confess that Jesus Christ is Lord (Phil. 2:11). The Christian church summarized its experience of Jesus Christ in the one word, *Lord*.

In recognizing Jesus as Lord, they prayed to him. Dying Stephen offered two prayers directly to Jesus in heaven: "Lord Jesus, receive my spirit" and "Lord, lay not this sin to their charge" (Acts 7:59–60). Paul prayed to Jesus in 2 Cor. 12:8 and Acts 22:8–18. Ananias talked with the Lord and then went to lay hands on Paul. "Brother Saul," he said, "the Lord has sent me—Jesus himself" (Acts 9:17, TEV). Praying to Jesus was the distinguishing mark of a disciple enabling their persecutors to identify them as shown in Acts 9:14,21.

The following Scriptures agree with this established custom of praying to Jesus: "Arise and be baptized, . . . calling on the name of the Lord" (Acts 22:16) and "For whosoever shall call upon the name of the Lord shall be saved" (Rom. 10:13). B. H. Carroll says it won't do to limit these to initial invocations connected with baptism or the first confession. These prayers to Jesus distinguished the early Christians throughout their lives, as appears from Paul's address: "Unto the church of God which is at Corinth, to them that are sanctified in Christ Jesus, called *to be* saints, with all that in every place call upon the name of Jesus Christ our Lord, both theirs and ours" (1 Cor. 1:2).

The history of the followers of Christ shows that they offered both prayer and praise to Christ. To deny that prayers should be offered to Christ denies that he is Lord.

The New Testament, however, does not record any prayers being offered to the Holy Spirit. This side simply offers the explanation that to insist it is wrong to pray to the Holy Spirit is to insist that he is not God.

The ascension of Jesus changed his ministry from one on earth to one in heaven. When he had been in the flesh, the disciples had him personally to consult. To know his will was to ask him. But Jesus told them a time was coming when they would not be able to ask him questions. "In that day ye shall ask me nothing" (John 16:23). Jesus would be away in heaven, but he wasn't going to leave us comfortless, without someone to ask. He promised another who would be our helper. The Holy Spirit is here on earth with us as our teacher to continue the work of Jesus. To deny that it is right to pray to this teacher is to deny his holiness, to deny that he is God. To pray to the Holy Spirit is praying to the God who is here with us, to the God we feel as we pray.

Neither side has a strong biblical passage which says, "You must pray to God the Father and to him only" or "You should pray to the Father, the Son, and the Holy Spirit." As long as we do not have that kind of biblical admonition, it will be up to us to decide from the evidence offered by both sides which is right for us.

We can spend our lives addressing our prayers only to the Father and have a perfectly acceptable prayer life. An intimacy with God can be experienced. Prayers will be answered, and the roles of Jesus and the Holy Spirit can be acknowledged in our praying without addressing them.

The other side, however, says that something is lost in acknowledging the roles when we cannot address them directly. Addressing Jesus and the Holy Spirit gives the pray-er a conscious recognition of their roles, quickening the pray-er's confidence in his communication. Each member of the Trinity performs a unique ministry; when we address Jesus or the Holy Spirit we are saying, "I appreciate what you do."

Bible teacher Lehman Strauss says:

> It is a perfectly natural and normal thing for any Christian to thank Jesus for dying for his sins. I have done this frequently in my own prayers. And why not? It was not the first nor the third Person in the Trinity who died on the cross. When I thank Jesus for shedding His blood for me, I address Him personally and directly.
>
> When I come to study the Bible, I ask the Holy Spirit to guide and teach me. I do not ask the Father or Jesus to do that for me which is the prescribed ministry of the Holy Spirit. For many years I have prayed in this way to the Holy Spirit, and the requests have been granted.[1]

Some Christians like to make their requests of Jesus because he was tempted as we are (Heb. 4:15). It's similar to sharing our troubles with someone who has experienced or is experiencing what we are going through. We want a sympathetic ear; we want to talk to someone who will understand. Because Jesus walked this earth as a person and knew our kinds of problems, we feel a kinship with him and feel free to ask what's on our hearts.

Now, after looking at both sides of the question, has anybody's mind been changed about who to pray to? Not if what my sociology professor said is true, but that's all right. The real help in our prayer lives is not going to come by continuing to discuss who we pray to, for there's something of much greater concern behind this issue. There's another question that needs to be asked: Is the name I use to address God a meaningful one, and is it expressed in a meaningful way?

When I work with small groups, I like to ask them who they pray to. One of the more frequent answers is "Lord." Then, I ask, "By *Lord* do you mean God the Father or Jesus?" When a long pause follows, as it often does, I'm tempted to wonder if the person has ever really thought about who he is praying to. Is he really conscious of the other presence when he prays? Certainly, Lord could mean Father or Jesus for the pray-er, but the fact that he doesn't know indicates that he may be using the name unthinkingly and without meaning.

God. Father. Jesus. Holy Spirit. Christ. Lord. Jehovah. God has many names. Is the one we use in our prayers meaningful to us?

Not many Christians would feel comfortable with Jehovah because God is much more personal to us than that name implies. Some Christians are uncomfortable using Father because of the memories they have of their own father. Because of their backgrounds, Father for them may be associated with fear and repulsion, anger and hostility, and sometimes even hate and scorn. Until they can be set free from these feelings, they might be more comfortable using another name for God.

Which name we use is not as important as how we use it. Sometimes we get so repetitious and singsongy in our praying that we are not even conscious of the name we are using. Sometimes God's name is no more than a prayer punctuation mark. "God, we thank you, God. God, as we gather here today, God, we ask you to help us study, God. We need you, God." Sometimes we do this because we pray too fast. When we do, we are not only not hallowing his name; we are not hallowing his presence.

As we choose meaningful names to address God, we need to express them in a meaningful way. The more names we know, the more we will know of his nature, and the greater consciousness we'll have of God when we pray. One pray-er who lives in a house with a fantastic view of God's creation said, "I never once pray in front of my picture window when I do not begin with 'Heavenly Father, Precious Son, O Holy Spirit . . .' I never fail to be moved by the work of God as Creator. Yet it would be no more than beautiful scenery for me if Christ had not come and if I did not feel the Spirit's presence with me. All of God surrounds me, and it takes more than one name to express how I feel."

Jesus himself gives us a poignant example of what it means to use God's name in prayer in John 17. This can best be seen by reading the entire chapter. Jesus begins with "Father, the hour is come," but he does not continue with simply Father; nor does he use it with every thought. He uses "O Father" and "Holy Father" and "O righteous Father" as is appropriate for what he is saying. One modern translation has exclamation marks sometimes following Father in this prayer; does that say something about the intensity with which Jesus spoke God's name? Jesus fully recognized the nature of the one to whom he was praying and appropriately expressed his name.

Hallowing God's name should permeate all of our living, but hallowing it in our prayers is an appropriate place to begin. The question, then, about God's name is not *Is it right or is it wrong?* but *Is it meaningful, and do I express it with meaning?*

Note

1. Lehman Strauss, *Sense and Nonsense about Prayer* (Chicago: Moody Press, 1974), p. 121.

9. What Does It Mean to Ask "in the Name of Jesus"?

It seems most appropriate that we follow the discussion of how we begin our prayers (what name we call God) with a discussion of how we end our prayers. Many of us would not think of ending our prayers without that important phrase "in the name of Jesus." We use those words because Jesus taught us to pray in his name.

"And whatsoever ye shall ask in my name, that will I do" (John 14:13).

"If ye shall ask any thing in my name, I will do *it*" (John 14:14).

"Ye have not chosen me, but I have chosen you, . . . that whatsoever ye shall ask of the Father in my name, he may give it you" (John 15:16).

"Whatsoever ye shall ask the Father in my name, he will give *it* you" (John 16:23).

"Hitherto have ye asked nothing in my name: ask, and ye shall receive, that your joy may be full" (John 16:24).

At first glance, the promises look too good to be true. "What we will"; "Anything"; "Whatsoever we ask" can be ours as long as we pray in the name of Jesus. Sounds simple enough, we reason. Sure, we can add "in the name of Jesus" to our requests, and he'll answer and give us what we ask for. But it doesn't take long, praying in this manner, to realize that there must be more to these promises than a casual reading would indicate. The simple voicing of the phrase in our prayers does not guarantee answers.

A similar interpretation regards "in the name of Jesus" as some kind of magic formula that grants us a hearing with God. Without the phrase, God will not even hear the request, let alone grant it. Indeed, one person writing to the editor of a Christian magazine about an article which had previously appeared said, "No wonder the person did not receive an answer to her prayer. Doesn't she know that every prayer must end with 'in Jesus' name' or God will not hear it?"

Perhaps it was this kind of reasoning that led us to the practice of ending our prayers with "in Jesus' name," but that makes using the phrase a superstitious kind of observance. We have more confidence in our words and our approach than we do in the God who answers.

To counteract superficial interpretations of praying in Jesus' name, explanations are given that are hard to understand and even harder to apply. Take this explanation, for example. "We pray in the name of Jesus when we rely on the redemption that he has wrought for us, when we have the spirit of Christ and seek the things which he seeks, and when we are in vital union with him."

And here's another one, equally as difficult to understand and apply. "Praying in the name of Christ signifies prayer in the name or character of Christ involving the elimination from our supplications of all that is foreign to his nature, and the inclusion of all those virtues and ideals he taught and exemplified—in a word, it is prayer in the holy and obedient spirit of Jesus."

Ideally and technically, these two interpretations are correct; but they offer little encouragement to pray. How many of us feel like we are in vital union with Christ when we come to pray? None of us deliberately wants to disregard the redemption he wrought for us, but many of our petitions seem very selfish and insignificant when compared to what he suffered. We would like to come in the obedient spirit of Jesus, but more often we come clothed in desperation. Sometimes it's all we can do to make ourselves pray, let alone be holy in our appearance.

On the one hand, "in the name of Jesus" is used superficially, giving us no real help with our praying. On the other hand, prayer is lifted above us—couched in words we do not understand and offering standards so high that we can never live up to them. Surely Jesus did not mean for his promises to be interpreted either way.

Some of the most tender, most considerate things Jesus said are found in the passages where he taught us to pray in his name (John 14; 15; 16). The occasion was the approaching of Jesus' death. The disciples were going to be shocked, shattered, and alone in a hostile world. Noting the circumstances, it seems a little superfluous to think Jesus was telling his disciples they could have anything they wanted if they tagged every prayer with his name. The words must have been an encouragement, a hope they could understand, in the days ahead. What, then, is the encouragement? What does it mean to ask in Jesus' name?

The phrase "in the name of" was not new to the disciples. In biblical usage, the expression *the name* is used in a very special way. It does not mean simply the name by which a person is addressed or called, such as John or Sam. It means the whole nature and character of the person insofar as it can be known. When the Bible says, "And they that know thy name will put their trust in thee" (Ps. 9:10) it does not mean that those who know what God is *called* will trust him. It means that those who know what God is *like*, those who know the character and the nature of God, will be willing to put their trust in him. The phrase "in the name of" sounds strange to our ears, but it did not sound strange to the ears of the disciples. They knew that to ask in Jesus' name was to ask for things in line with his character and nature.

For us to fully understand what it means to ask for what is in line with the character and nature of Jesus, let's examine his promises without their famous phrase. "And whatsoever ye shall ask, that will I do." "If ye shall ask anything, I will do it." "Whatsoever ye shall ask of the Father, he may give it you." If Jesus had stated his promises in this manner, he would have been giving believers unlimited power. Anything could be ours. No limit. No ceiling could be put on our requests. No bounds on the power. That kind of power would be a very big responsibility. Could we really be trusted with "anything" and "whatsoever"? What we will may not always be right or best. How would we keep our selfish natures from completely taking over and getting what we want?

We can't be trusted with that kind of power. Christians are not to have everything. Jesus said to ask in his name to show us that there is a limit to what we should ask for. There is a limit to the power we have in prayer. Only those things we can ask for in his name, in accordance with the character and nature of Jesus, can we expect to receive.

Here's an illustration that's often used to help us understand the limitation. When we present a check to be cashed at the bank with someone else's name on the check other than ours, we are asking in his name. It does not matter whether we have money in the bank or not. If the person whose name is signed to the check has money there, the check will be cashed. There's going to be a limit, however, to how much money we can receive according to what the other person, in whose name we are acting, has in his account. No matter how much money he has in the bank, it will still be a finite amount. The amount of his deposit will limit the amount we can receive. If he has a thousand dollars in the bank, we can draw fifty or five hundred or one thousand dollars, but not over that. We could not get one thousand dollars and five cents. The check we cash in another man's name cannot go beyond what he has on deposit.

Likewise, there's a limit to what we may rightfully ask and expect from God. "In the name of Jesus" is that limitation. What is in accordance with the nature and character of Jesus is what we have on deposit. That's what we can ask and expect to receive.

To believers Jesus says, "Ask. Do ask, and you will receive what you need to live the Christian life. But you can't have all power. There is good power and bad power. I must limit you so that you won't get mixed up or defeated in this earthly life. For your sake, I need to be in control. Ask for those things which are in line with my nature, in line with who I am and what I have done. Ask, and those things will not be refused you."

If praying in Jesus' name is a limitation, doesn't that take away from Jesus' promises to answer? Doesn't that dilute them? How could a limitation be an encouragement?

Praying in Jesus' name is a broad limitation that upon closer examination encourages our asking just as much as Jesus intended for us to. Considering all that Jesus was and is, it's the broadest limitation we'll ever find.

Whatever prayer has to do with sin, God will answer because Jesus paid the price of sin once and for all. Sin is conquerable. So Jesus is saying, "Ask, that your sins may be forgiven, remembering that I've already paid the price for them."

Is our prayer regarding temptation? Ask with confidence for the ability to resist, knowing that Jesus resisted. And "because greater is he that is in you, than he that is in the world" (1 John 4:4), we can overcome temptation.

Is our prayer request concerning a "hopeless" situation? From all appearances, as far as we can see, there is no possible solution. In our despair, we can ask because Jesus is hope (1 Tim. 1:1). He can make a difference in any situation.

Is our request concerning something of a physical nature—pain, sickness, etc.? We can take it to Jesus, the Great Physician. We can remember how he opened his arms to the blind and the lame when he was on this earth. We can remember and pray for ourselves and for others because it is Jesus' nature to heal.

Is our request concerning someone's salvation or for a missionary or for an evangelist? We can pray fervently and expectantly because Jesus came to seek and to save the lost (Luke 19:10).

Are we bothered with daily cares, worrying over troublesome things? Remember that Jesus turned the water into wine to save a couple's marriage party from being ruined (John 2:1–11). The couple would have been embarrassed and humiliated if they had run out of wine. To prevent that, Jesus put forth his power in sympathy, in kindness, and in understanding. How comforting to know that Jesus with all his power and wisdom is concerned about the small details of life.

The limitation of asking in the name of Jesus is an encouragement when we consider all that Jesus was and did and is. The more we know of Jesus, his life, his aims, his purposes, and his conduct, the freer we will be to ask. We'll see what he has placed on deposit for us to claim in his name. Asking in Jesus' name is a limitation; there are unholy things we should not have. At the same time, what we can ask for within this limitation is infinite because of the inexhaustible nature of Jesus Christ.

Occasionally, though, we may have trouble discerning what requests fit under his name and what requests do not fit. Now, if Jesus were present, we could just ask him: Lord, is this something you would approve of? The mother of Zebedee's children came and said, "Lord, I want to ask you something." "What do you want?" Jesus asked her. "Promise me that these two sons of mine will sit at your right and your left when you are king." Jesus had to tell her that her request was out of place. Her request was not his to grant, but Jesus was there to explain.

Now he is away, and we want to know if a prayer request is in accordance with his nature. Jesus is not here for us to ask, but his Spirit is. The Holy Spirit is on earth here as our teacher continuing the work of Jesus. When Jesus was here, he taught his disciples how to pray and what to pray for. The Holy Spirit now teaches us what to pray for. The counselor whom the Father sent in Jesus' name continues and completes the teaching ministry of Jesus. If we want to know if a request is characteristic of Jesus, we can seek the guidance of the Holy Spirit.

Being obedient Christians will also help us know what is characteristic of Jesus. A corollary to the promises to answer prayers prayed in Jesus' name is John 15:7: "If ye abide in me, and my words abide in you, ye shall ask what ye will and it shall be done unto you." Abiding in Jesus is defined as keeping his commandments (John 15:10). The abiding-in-Christ Christian seeks to do what

Jesus taught. He takes the principles Jesus taught and attempts to live by them; and in so doing, he comes to know Jesus (1 John 2:3). The obedient Christian becomes like Jesus and acts in situations as Jesus would act. He takes on the nature of Jesus.

Andrew Murray says that when the name of Jesus becomes the power that rules our lives, its power in prayer will be seen, too. Praying in Jesus' name, he says, is a spiritual power which no one can use further than he obtains the capacity for, by living and acting in that name.

The disciples lived and acted in the name of Jesus, but they had been with him. They knew from firsthand experience what his nature was like. They were there when Jesus healed the blind, the lepers, the cripples. They were there when he cast out demons and raised the dead. They knew what the nature of Jesus was because they had spent time with him, and that is exactly what we must do. He's not here in the flesh for us to spend time with, but we can know him by studying the pages of the book that reveals his nature.

We must find out for ourselves what Jesus is like, and we can find out all about him in God's Word. We must study it so thoroughly that his words remain in us (John 15:7)—stick with us to ever remind us of what his nature is like. Studying the Gospels is an appropriate place to begin, but all of the Bible will give witness to the nature of God's Son.

The more we know of Jesus' nature—through the Holy Spirit, through obedience, and through study—the easier it will be to pray in his name. These three things intermingle in our lives until we can ask confidently and boldly in his nature. Our awareness of all that Jesus is increases as the Holy Spirit leads us, as we grow in obedience, and as our knowledge expands. There will always be more of Jesus' nature to learn, but we can always respond with the knowledge we presently have of his nature.

We can better understand this by contrasting the requests of a two-year-old with a teenager's requests. A two-year-old will not be discriminatory in his requests; he wants everything! He does not know yet what is right and wrong. All he knows is that Mom and Dad are his sources for getting. He responds accordingly by asking for everything.

But a teenager should not be asking for everything. Because he has heard his parents say no on a number of occasions, because he has learned through obedience, and because he has experienced their teachings concerning behavior, he'll know better than to ask for some things. Did that make it wrong for him to ask when we was two? No, at two he was responding to all he knew of the parents' will at that time.

As a child grows, he is expected to ask more wisely. Occasionally he may slip and make an inappropriate request. The parents answer, "You know better than to ask that." What the parents are really saying is, "After all we have taught you, after living together these many years, after having our answer on this same question before, why are you asking?" Are the parents displeased that the child has actually made the request? No, they are disappointed that the child still has not perceived their nature and will.

Some of us are two years old in our prayer lives. We throw out all kinds of requests, hoping for some of them to be answered and never really being confident that God will answer. Others of us are more like the teenager. Occasionally we slip; but for the most part, we can discern what is right and what is not right to ask. Others of us may be far beyond that. We pray with expectancy, confident that God will answer because we know how to ask. The longer we are led of the Spirit, the more we obey, the more we study, the greater our knowledge of the nature of Jesus will be.

Because we are all at different "ages" in our knowledge of Jesus, it appears that some Christians have more requests answered than others. If some do, it's because they know what to ask. They are keenly aware of who Jesus is, so they know what to ask and what to rightfully expect to receive.

Praying in Jesus' name is not a matter of taking a rigorous account of each request before we speak it. Is this in his name? Is this one? Is this? The inward impressions of the Holy Spirit confirmed through our obedience and study intermingle in such a way in our lives that we take on the nature of Jesus. His nature will permeate our lives so that we can open our mouths and let the requests come forth. The words "in the name of Jesus" need not even be uttered in one's prayers; the nature of our requests reveals whether they are in accordance with the nature and likeness of Jesus.

10. Does God Answer the Prayers of Those Who Do Not Know Jesus?

One problem in finding a biblical answer to the question of whether God answers the prayers of non-Christians is the term *Christian*. We do not have the term appearing in the Bible until Acts 11:26, when the disciples were first called Christians at Antioch. But of course, Old Testament personalities who were believers could not be termed non-Christians. That part of the Bible which follows Acts 11 does not record very many specific prayers for us to examine to enable us to see how God responds to the prayers of non-Christians.

But God has always had a people, a group bound by a covenant to following him, just as Christians are committed to following. In terms of the covenant, there were those within the fold and those without. To see what response is made to the petitions of both non-Christians and believers in God who lived before Jesus' earthly life, we can look at how God the Father and God the Son responded to the petitions from those outside the covenant. In some incidents, especially in the life of Jesus, it is hard to tell; but here are some that are generally regarded as prayers coming from those outside the fold.

Hagar (Gen. 16:1–15)
In the Old Testament, we see God hearing the affliction (the need was not even verbalized) of Hagar, an Egyptian.

After being dealt harshly with by her mistress, Sarai, Abram's wife, she fled to the wilderness where an angel of God met her. "And the angel of the Lord said unto her, Behold, thou *art* with child, and shalt bear a son, and shalt call his name Ishmael; because the Lord hath heard thy affliction" (Gen. 16:11).

Manasseh (2 Chron. 33:1–20)

Manasseh makes a good example of how a wicked man turns to God when in distress. He had access to the covenant, but he separated himself from it by not doing God's will. To say he was very evil would be putting it mildly. He erected altars to other gods; he incorporated astral worship; and he even sacrificed his own sons. He practiced soothsaying and sorcery and dealt with mediums and with wizards. Besides making Judah sin extensively by the things he introduced and promoted, Manasseh caused so much innocent blood to be shed that it filled Jerusalem from one end to another (2 Kings 21:16).

God tried to speak to Manasseh about what he was doing, but Manasseh refused to listen. The commanders of the Assyrian army invaded Judah. They captured Manasseh, stuck hooks in him, put him in chains, and took him to Babylon. In his suffering he turned to the Lord and begged him for help. God accepted Manasseh's prayer and answered it by letting him go back to Jerusalem and rule again. The wonderful result of this was "Then Manasseh knew that the Lord he *was* God" (2 Chron. 33:13) and devoted the rest of his reign to reform.

The Heathen Mariners (Jonah 1)

When the storm first hit the ship going to Tarshish with Jonah aboard, the heathen mariners were afraid. Each cried to his god. Their gods didn't answer, and the storm continued. They tried throwing things overboard to lighten the ship, and still they were unsafe. Even after Jonah told them that their problem would be solved if they threw him overboard, the men still tried hard to bring the ship back to land and escape the storm. But they could not. "Wherefore they cried unto the Lord, and said, We beseech thee, O Lord, we beseech thee, let us not perish for this man's life, and lay not upon us innocent blood: for thou, O Lord, hast done as it pleased thee. So they took up Jonah, and cast him forth into the sea: and the sea ceased from her raging" (Jonah 1:14–15). Their safety so astonished the sailors that they promised to serve the Lord.

Capernaum Nobleman (John 4:46–53)

The Capernaum nobleman was a government official. His son was dying; and in his distress, the nobleman forgot his position of importance and traveled miles to ask Jesus to heal his son. Jesus' first statement wasn't exactly encouraging to the nobleman; but perhaps Jesus was speaking for the sake of the crowd when he said, "Except ye see signs and wonders, ye will not believe" (John 4:48). Nevertheless, the nobleman persisted; he pleaded with Jesus to return home with him before his son died. Jesus told him to go back home, for his son would live. And just as Manasseh's answered prayer changed the course of his life, so did Jesus' answer change the nobleman's. The result was that the nobleman and his whole household believed.

Syrophoenician Woman (Matt. 15:21–28; Mark 7:24–30)

Like the nobleman, the Syrophoenician woman came because of her child. Her daughter had an evil spirit in her. The woman was a Gentile who persisted in getting help from Jesus even after he told her that he was sent only to the lost sheep of Israel. Jesus recognized faith in her persistence and granted her wish of healing for her daughter.

Thief on the Cross (Luke 23:39-43)

Jesus was crucified between two known criminals. The one who defended Jesus against the insults of the other one said to him, "Lord, remember me when thou comest into thy kingdom" (Luke 23:42). And Jesus told him that "To day shalt thou be with me in paradise" (Luke 23:43).

Cornelius (Acts 10)

Cornelius was close to the fold of God. He was a God-fearer, a Gentile who attached himself to the Jewish religion without accepting circumcision and the law. He prayed and he gave alms; but the Jews still regarded him as a Gentile, as Peter was quick to point out when he went to Cornelius' house. Nevertheless, God responded to the prayers of Cornelius. God's angel said to him, "Thy prayers and thine alms are come up for a memorial before God" (Acts 10:4). God's response to Cornelius' prayers opened the door for Gentiles to become part of the Christian church.

"O thou that hearest prayer, unto thee shall all flesh come," said the psalmist (Ps. 65:2), and that is exactly what the Bible shows us happening. All flesh, all kinds come to God with petitions. Therefore, from these examples, we have to acknowledge that God has, at times, answered the prayers of those outside the fold and would respond in the same way to the prayers of non-Christians today.

Some of us may feel threatened by this acknowledgment. "If sin is a barrier to prayer, how can a sinner pray and be heard?" "Non-Christians haven't made any kind of profession of faith; they don't deserve to have their prayers answered." "It isn't fair to Christians for God to anwer those outside the fold."

A basic Old Testament thought is that God does not hear the prayers of bad men. "If I regard iniquity in my heart, the Lord will not hear *me*" (Ps. 66:18), said the psalmist. When Job was speaking of the hypocrite, he said, "Will God hear his cry when trouble cometh upon him?" (Job 27:9). Ezekiel said of the disobedient people: "Though they cry in mine ears with a loud voice, *yet* will I not hear them" (Ezek. 8:18).

This idea is also picked up in the New Testament. A blind man healed by Jesus expressed this idea in defending him. The Pharisees were accusing Jesus of being a sinner. The blind man reminded the Pharisees of a principle with which they were already familiar: "Now we know that God heareth not sinners: but if any man be a worshipper of God, and doeth his will, him he heareth" (John 9:31). Peter quoted from a psalm to express this same idea (compare 1 Pet. 3:12 with Ps. 34:15–16).

These verses are not aimed for those outside the fold. The admonition is for those in the covenant, the Old and the New. The truth in the idea is not that a certain degree of badness automatically turns God's ear away from us. The truth is that sin keeps us from being appropriate receivers of what God wants to give.

Under the ministry of Isaiah, there were those within the covenant who believed that God no longer answered prayer. They were saying, "He answered prayer in Elijah's day, but he isn't doing it now. His arm is no longer mighty; his ear has become dull of hearing." But the prophet Isaiah said, "Behold, the Lord's hand is not shortened, that it cannot save; neither his ear heavy, that it cannot hear: But your iniquities have separated between you and your God, and your sins have hid *his* face from you, that he will not hear" (Isa. 59:1–2).

The sins the people had committed had cut off their communication. God cannot work through clogged channels. It is to the man who keeps his commandments that God reveals himself. His people cannot be immoral and expect God to work through them. His people cannot commit injustices without raising a barrier that blocks effective communication. Sin and its effects can pile up in a Christian's life until he loses his sensitivity to God's voice and no longer even wants to pray. Sin is a barrier to prayer for those committed to following God.

Sin is also a barrier for non-Christians. Even if we were to proclaim to them that God answers their prayers, non-Christians wouldn't immediately bombard heaven with requests. The sin that separates them from a personal relationship with God is there, looming large and insurmountable in their lives, and keeps them from praying. That's why many non-Christians would never utter a prayer until they are hurting badly as the Capernaum nobleman or desperate like Manasseh. As one man who had been adrift at sea with two companions for twenty-one days said, "I was never a religious person. I grew up a book-educated, New York cynic. But when the chips were down, we got down on our knees together, looked up at the enormous universe surrounding us—and we prayed."

Even if the non-Christian temporarily surmounts the hurdle of sin and God answers his petition, the sin is still going to be there. One answered prayer does not make him a Christian. As Jesus said, "No man cometh unto the Father, but by me" (John 14:6). The non-Christian with one or two or even more answered prayers still needs the redeeming power of Jesus Christ in order to have that sin taken care of once and for all and in order to enjoy a personal relationship with God.

As long as a person remains unredeemed, outside the fold, he can never know the kind of prayer life that a Christian may enjoy. The non-Christian speaks as a stranger to God. A Christian speaks intimately with God. He prays knowing God wants to answer. He knows God wants to bless him and uses prayer as the channel to receive those blessings.

There is a rich inheritance available for every Christian that a non-Christian cannot even comprehend or ever hope to enjoy as long as he remains outside the fold. So we should never feel that it is out of place for God to answer the prayers of non-Christians. William Barclay says:

> God has two kinds of sons, the sons who break his heart and the sons who delight his heart, and there are precious things for those who do their Father's will . . . there are things for the obedient son that the disobedient son can never know, until he turns and submits to his Father's love.[1]

That God sometimes answers the prayers of non-Christians does not contradict the fact that sin is a barrier to effective prayer. Neither will an answered petition save a non-Christian; accepting Jesus is the only way. A non-Christian can never enjoy the kind of prayer life that a Christian can experience. These facts should not threaten us; rather, if we will let them, they can be a boon to us. Believing that God sometimes answers the prayers of non-Christians can help us with our witnessing, with teaching our children to pray, and with our asking.

Sometimes, in our witnessing, we find ourselves in situations where the ABC plan of salvation or the Four Spiritual Laws don't quite fit. Pat Boone had just such an encounter with a Jewish pornographer in the steam room at the Sands Hotel in Las Vegas. The pornographer brought up Pat Boone's book *A New Song* in the presence of several other guys. Boone was apprehensive, fearful that he was being set up for a joke. Boone describes Ace, the pornographer, as the last guy in Las Vegas he would share his testimony with. Ace describes himself as his own worst enemy, four-times married, twice-bankrupt, ashamed of the junk he sells, fat, flabby, over forty, headed for a gallbladder operation, and scared. Here's how Boone handled it after Ace insisted that Boone pray for him.

> "I'll be happy to pray for you. I will. But you know, God wants to hear from you about your problems. That's really the whole idea. Will you pray, too?"
>
> The look on his face seemed a mixture of sadness and hilarity . . . The twin forces rushed together and erupted into a loud laugh, as he said, "Me? *Pray?* Oh, come *on*—God would strike me dead, tell me to get lost or go to hell, or something! You gotta be kidding!"
>
> . . . .
>
> "Ace," I said, obeying an inner impulse before I quite realized how rash it was, "so many people have the wrong idea about prayer and about God Himself. He's not interested in just hearing religious words from so-called religious people. Jesus Himself said there was only one really *good* person— and that was God! So God wants to hear from each of us, not because we're good, but because He just plain ol' *loves* us!
>
> . . . .
>
> "Tell you what—I've never suggested this to anybody, but I'm going to pray that God *will be real to you in some way that you'll recognize!* I don't know what He'll do, but I believe He'll show you in some way that He hears you, and that you're getting through. Will you pray for the same thing?"
>
> "I don't know how to pray, Boone—I really don't." He

looked a little uneasy, suddenly aware of the unbelieving stares of the others.

"I don't mean right here, now," I said, "but later, when you're alone. You don't have any trouble talking to *me*, do you?"

Ace grinned, a little relieved, maybe. "No—but you're not God!"

"That's right, I'm not, and it's a good thing for you! But you can talk to Him just like you're talking to me. The words just don't matter, because He's listening to your heart anyway. You just need to keep in mind *who* you're talking to. It's important, though, that *you* speak to Him—and I will, too. Will you do it?"

"Okay. I'll try it, but—I don't know." [2]

When Boone's engagement came down to its last performance, he went back to the steam room one last time. While there, he received a phone call from Ace.

As I went to pick up the receiver, I couldn't help wondering if I'd been set up for an elaborate joke, and this was the punch line.

The excitement on the other end of the line quickly erased the thought. "Your prayers are *answered!* YOUR PRAYERS ARE ANSWERED!" The voice was so loud I had to hold the phone away from my ear!

"Hold on, Ace," I squeezed the words in edgewise. "What's happened? What do you mean?"

"Boone! You know you said to just talk to God like I was talking to you? And to ask Him to show me something? Well, I thought you were probably crazy, but I did it. I mean, I talked right out loud, like you said. I really felt like I was talking to the lamp or the air, and I didn't think my words were gettin' outta the room—but I did it.

"And you must have been praying, too—right?"

I chuckled, "I sure was!"

"Well, *lemme tell you what happened!*

"I went in today for my last examination before the gallbladder operation. I was scared to death. The doc gave me this chalky stuff to drink and then X-rayed me. In a little

> while he came in with the X-rays and just shaking his head—
> he said he *couldn't find the stones!*
>
> *"The gallstones are gone!*
>
> "The doc says he can't operate on me when he can't find the stones!"
>
> I was numb—I *really* was. "That's fantastic, Ace!"
>
> "Yeah—but what do I do now?" [3]

Boone told Ace to get a modern translation of the Bible and start reading about the one who had answered his prayer. Some, those who do not believe God sometimes answers the prayers of non-Christians, would say that God was answering Pat Boone's prayer and not Ace's. The point of the illustration is not whose prayer was answered, but to show us how Boone could witness and encourage Ace because he believed God wants to hear from everyone.

If God doesn't answer the prayers of non-Christians, we are in an awkward position when it comes to teaching our children to pray. The best time to teach them to pray openly and honestly is in their early years. It would be very difficult to teach praying without teaching expectancy of answers. In many cases, the faith of little children as expressed in their expectancy to receive boosts the faith of the parents.

If we believe God does not answer the prayers of non-Christians, and at the same time we teach our unsaved children to pray, how are we going to explain the answers they receive? Would an appropriate time be after they become Christians? "Look, son, now that you've become a Christian you can really pray and God will answer you. Before, we were only learning about prayer; and the answers you received were coincidences. Now that you've become a Christian, the answers you receive will really be God's answers." To be sure, once the child becomes a Christian, his prayer life will take on a new dimension; but that's not to negate the prayer experiences he previously had. One builds on the other.

Acknowledging the mercy that God shows in answering the prayers of non-Christians not only helps us with our witnessing and with our children; but it can help us with our asking. Pray-ers seem to be haunted by the idea that we have to be so good to have our prayers answered or that we have to fulfill a number of requirements first. If we were questioned about having to be good enough to have our prayers answered, we would deny it; but it's in our hearts, in our praying, where we are bothered by it. We are particularly bothered when an especially desired answer is not forthcoming. We browbeat ourselves and wonder what we are doing wrong.

Corresponding to the Jews' belief that God does not hear the prayers of a bad man, they believed he did hear the prayers of the good man. "The Lord is far from the wicked, but he heareth the prayer of the righteous" (Prov. 15:29). The psalmist said that one who approaches God must have clean hands and a pure heart (Ps. 24:3–4). If we waited until our hands were completely clean and our hearts completely pure, we would never be able to pray. Some of the most humbling experiences I've had as a Christian has been after some sin has been pulled by its roots out of my heart, and I look back over the time that it was so firmly implanted and see how merciful God was to answer my requests. Sometimes I was aware of the sin being there; sometimes I wasn't. But in each case, once it was removed, I could only marvel at God's mercy in his continual response to me.

Sin can pile up in our lives until our channel for communication is clogged. We should work against that happening. At the same time, we in ourselves can never remove all the sin from our lives so that we may approach God with a pure heart. That's why we need Jesus, so he can be our righteousness. None of us, Christian or non-Christian, are ever good enough to have our prayers answered. In the end, both of us depend upon God's mercy and grace.

If there is known sin in our lives, blocking our channel, let's get on with removing it. If that has been taken care of, and the answer is still not forthcoming, let's not browbeat ourselves. Instead, let's remember who we are praying to.

The God we pray to is the same God who heard and answered terrible, horrible Manasseh. He is the same God who answered a dying thief's prayer, who heard the affliction of an Egyptian woman crying in the wilderness, and who responded to the cry of terrified heathen mariners. Let's trust him and not our goodness. Asking is not a matter of building up our case or meeting all the requirements. Asking is giving God the channel he needs to reveal to us what he's always longed for us to know, that he is a God of love, mercy, and grace.

Notes

1. William Barclay, *The Beatitudes and the Lord's Prayer for Everyman* (New York: Harper and Row, 1968), pp. 170–71.
2. Pat Boone, *A Miracle a Day Keeps the Devil Away* (Old Tappan: Fleming H. Revell, 1974), pp. 42–43.
3. Ibid., pp. 43–44.

11. Why Pray with Others? Isn't Praying Alone Enough?

"Why should we pray aloud together?" asked a young person. "It says right here in black and white that we should go into our closet to pray." He was pointing to Matthew 6:6: "Enter into thy closet, and . . . pray to thy Father which is in secret."

In that verse, Jesus was warning us against praying for the approval of others. Jesus also said, "Again I say unto you, That if two of you shall agree on earth as touching any thing that they shall ask, it shall be done for them of my Father which is in heaven. For where two or three are gathered together in my name, there am I in the midst of them" (Matt. 18:19-20).

And James said, "Is any among you afflicted? let him pray. Is any merry? let him sing psalms. Is any sick among you? let him call for the elders of the church; and let them pray over him, anointing him with oil in the name of the Lord: And the prayer of faith shall save the sick, and the Lord shall raise him up; and if he have committed sins, they shall be forgiven him. Confess *your* faults one to another, and pray one for another, that ye may be healed" (Jas. 5:13-16).

From the words of Jesus and James, we can find some special blessings reserved for Christians who pray together.

1. Jesus promises to be present when Christians pray together.

1. Jesus promises to be present when Christians pray together. This is not to say that he is not present when we pray alone; neither is it to say that his presence is felt at every group prayer meeting. Jesus' promise to be present when Christians pray together will be actualized when Christians claim that promise together.

People can meet in the same room and voice prayers without ever experiencing Christ's presence. This may happen when we've taken our privilege of prayer for granted, when its practice has become habitual. We need to realize anew that our God is living and personal, and the way we pray should be indicative of his holy presence. Very simply, we can begin our prayer time together by acknowledging his presence and his nature. More than one person needs to do this until the group is consciously aware of his presence. "Lord, we thank you that you are right here with us." "We thank you that we can each experience your presence at the same time." "We're glad you are a God who hears and answers prayers and that you are listening to what we have to say right now." Beginning the prayer time in this way acknowledges the Lord's presence and stimulates participants to remember who it is we're praying to.

Now, following this acknowledgment, if everyone starts praying long drawn-out prayers, the stimulus may fade. Fortunately, God's patience and listening ability extends far beyond ours, and he does not withdraw himself from us. But we withdraw ourselves from *conscious* awareness of him. We're at the meeting to pray, and our initiative to do so may be stymied while waiting for someone else to finish. We lose interest while someone else prays on and on.

When we pray together, it is best if we pray short prayers, addressing ourselves to one topic at a time, and then giving others a chance to pray for that same topic before going on to another. In this way, we are acknowledging the fact that we are *all* gathered to pray and not gathered to hear one person pray. This makes our prayer time a group conversation with the Lord. All of us can continue to claim his presence as we repeatedly get chances to address him directly.

2. In addition to promising his presence to those who pray together, Jesus also promises answers. Much of the work God calls us to do is corporate activity; God needs the abilities and energies of people working together in order to accomplish his work. To ask together gives God the group channel he needs. The reality of God working among us in this way confirms our personal faith in an invisible God.

It is with regard to having a corporate will that the words "if two of you agree" are significant. The channel will be blocked if we are not in agreement. The promised answers will not come. Before we pray together, we would do well to ask ourselves, *What is it that we expect God to do in response to our request?* Our answers will reveal what it is we are willing to let God do through us and reveal whether or not we are in agreement.

3. In response to our sense of awareness of Christ's presence and his promise to answer, we express ourselves. We let our feelings be known. Our needs, our confessions, and our thanksgivings are expressed. Consequently, through this type of sharing, we learn to know our fellow Christians in a way not possible through other kinds of group activities.

As we talk together with the Lord in prayer, we have to be honest in acknowledgment of who he is. There is no hiding with him. Our spiritual masks that we sometimes carry to Sunday School and church to protect ourselves from embarrassment or hurt fall away when we come into Christ's presence. The self-protective barriers we erect disappear, and our true selves are revealed.

As often as I have experienced this dropping of the masks, I never cease to be amazed by it. Christians, whose personalities I thought I could not tolerate, change when we pray together. Haughty Christians become humble. Loud talkers pray softly. The domineering become other-oriented and weep prayerfully for someone else. Love permeates the group and irritations disappear. (We must also realize here that maybe something happens to the writer when she prays. Maybe she has a mask that is dropped, enabling her to see others in a different light.)

If this dropping of the spiritual masks does not occur in our prayer group, maybe some self-examination is in order. Do we as a group really claim Christ's presence? If he is present, we must be ourselves. That's characteristic of Jesus' nature. When we meet him face to face, we see ourselves as we really are.

If we are claiming his presence then and still feel uncomfortable about expressing ourselves, maybe the participants are the problem. Is our group small enough so that everyone feels comfortable about participating? Is our group a confidential one? Have we agreed to speak to no one outside the group about our requests, and is that agreement being kept? Have we created a climate of honesty, where we can be free to express our doubts and struggles without fear of rebuke? If a small number of us really claim Christ's presence and commit ourselves to one another, allowing for honesty and trust, we can learn to know our fellow Christians through praying together in a way not possible through other kinds of group activities.

4. While we're praying together, dropping those spiritual masks, we learn a lot about our fellow Christians.

We learn what they are enduring. Rosalind Rinker says, "Before I learned the secret of praying together, I thought that my burdens were greater than anyone else's burdens." [1]

Left alone to our own private praying, we become very "I" centered. *My* requests, *my* problems, *my* desires, *my* difficulties fill our prayers. When we pray with others we become aware of the rest of the body of Christ and *their* problems, *their* sufferings, etc. Much to our surprise, we may discover that some people have worse problems than we do. Some have great obstacles that must be tackled just to follow the Lord, let alone perform any great feats. We learn this about them when we pray with them, and we are helped by it. Our faith will be strengthened; and we'll be able to resist the devil, knowing that our fellow Christians in the world are also experiencing suffering (1 Pet. 5:9).

5. James assured us that physical *and spiritual* healing can take place as Christians pray together. This is not to say that healings cannot take place alone or under other circumstances. It is to say that praying together provides an atmosphere conducive to healing. Rosalind Rinker tells about having eight conference leaders pray together. She asked them to stand in a circle, holding hands for a few moments while they prayed.

> As we stood there, all taking part quietly, a professional woman of some renown suddenly spoke to a retired missionary. "I can't stand in this circle holding your hand without asking your forgiveness. Nor can I any longer conceal our violent disagreement." There was mutual admission, forgiveness and God's healing love.
>
> "As long as I didn't have to take her hand in prayer I could hide my hostility toward her," said the first woman, "but with the love active in this circle, I could no longer pretend. I had to let go—and let love take over." [2]

6. Praying with others is very important for those times when we cannot pray for ourselves. Sometimes we are too ill, too upset, or too distressed to pray. At those times, when we are beyond articulating our own needs, we need someone else to pray for us. We need them to do it in our presence, and we need to hear the prayer.

James said, "Call for the elders . . . and let them pray over him, anointing him with oil." While the elders could pray for the sick man out of his presence, James insisted on their coming to the actual scene. By praying within sight and hearing of the sufferer, the prayer is more likely to be heartfelt and fervent. But the greater benefit is for the sick man, that he may become conscious of the effective power of prayer uttered in faith. The coming of the elders, the tone of their voice, their presence, their words, and even their touch indicate hope to the sick man. Anyone can say, "I'll pray for you"; but to come to our sickbed and to actually ask God for our healing is a ministry of hope as well as a prayer of faith.

7. Praying with the sick and suffering is not the only occasion when audible praying by other Christians is meaningful. There are lots of occasions in the lives of Christians living and working together in which "I'll be remembering you in prayer" is simply not good enough. Maybe it's the nature of our work or the nature of the world in which we live, but there's something about saying good-bye to Christians as they go to new places of service that compels us to pray for them *in their presence*. The words are touching; the faith expressed is comforting; and there's a commissioning and a love expressed that is important to those going and to those staying.

After Jesus was gone, his followers needed direction as to what to do next. They met in the upper room and prayed (Acts 1:13–14). When they needed a successor to Judas, they prayed together (Acts 1:24-25). When Peter needed to be delivered from jail, they met at the house of John Mark's mother to pray (Acts 12:12). They praised God together (Acts 2:46-47). Paul and Silas prayed while in trouble together (Acts 16:25). Twice as Paul bid farewell to a group of believers, he prayed with them (Acts 20:36; 21:5). When we need guidance, when we need deliverance, when we suffer together, when we offer praise, when we say good-bye—these are occasions that call for praying aloud together.

8. Praying with others encourages us in our private praying. Our prayers and, in particular, our asking can be improved by praying with others.

Sharing our requests with others tests the suitability of our requests. "If two of you agree" is a good indicator as to the rightness of our request. Agreement is very important when the answer to the request is going to affect the whole group. If the others cannot agree with us about our request, we'd better question its appropriateness. Families, husbands and wives, need to be in agreement. If we cannot agree with our spouse and say, "Well, I'll just pray this through by myself," we'd better take a closer look at the request.

The answers we receive together from agreed-upon requests encourage us in making our requests when we pray alone. The experience of having God answer a group of pray-ers encourages us individually. Left to ourselves, we will experience doubt from time to time as long as we worship an invisible God. Seeing God's response to a group request removes doubt and is one more assurance of God's willingness to answer.

Praying with others helps us to be more other-oriented when we pray alone. As we get to know our fellow Christians, we grow to love them and care for them. We become conscious that all Christians are struggling, and we become more sensitive to the needs of Christians everywhere. We remember their needs and pray for them when we are alone.

Sometimes, when we pray with others, we become bold and ask for things we never intended asking for at all. That's part of feeling Christ's presence in a special way when we are in a group. We begin to believe as we have never believed before.

Also, in group praying, we hear the requests of others and note what they ask for. At first, their requests may even startle us. How could they be so bold? But as they ask and God answers, we gain courage and approach him boldly because we have heard others ask.

While it would be hard to biblically support a case for an imperative that *every* Christian should pray with others (what kind of prayer would a forced prayer be, anyway?), it is a highly recommended option. What the Bible says and the benefits we observe should make us want to pray with others. A pray-er may not experience all eight benefits every time he prays with others or every time he joins a prayer group, but he will find his own private prayers changed. His requests, his courage, his attitude, and his boldness will all be improved by having prayed with others.

Notes

1. Rosalind Rinker, *Prayer: Conversing with God* (Grand Rapids: Zondervan Publishing House, 1959), p. 36.
2. Rosalind Rinker, *Communicating Love Through Prayer* (Grand Rapids: Zondervan Publishing House, 1966), p. 89.

12. What Is the Real Tragedy of Paul's Thorn in the Flesh?

The apostle Paul was imprisoned, whipped, and often near death. As he himself said, "Five times I was given the thirty-nine lashes by the Jews; three times I was whipped by the Romans; and once I was stoned. I have been in three shipwrecks, and once I spent twenty-four hours in the water. In my many travels I have been in danger from floods and from robbers, in danger from fellow Jews and from Gentiles; there have been dangers in the cities, dangers in the wilds, dangers on the high seas, and dangers from false friends. There has been work and toil; often I have gone without sleep; I have been hungry and thirsty; I have often been without enough food, shelter, or clothing" (2 Cor. 11:24–27, TEV). None of us would be eager to trade places with a man like that, for his life was filled with tragedy.

One of the more talked about of Paul's tragedies is his thorn in the flesh. In 2 Corinthians 12:7–9, in which Paul talked about the thorn, his messenger from Satan, he didn't specifically say what it was. Christians have been wondering ever since.

Some Christians say the thorn was malaria because the Greek word for *thorn* could be interpreted as *stake*. The malaria fever in that region of the world was like a stake pounded into the forehead when it occurred. Others say it was the continual opposition and persecution Paul had to endure in preaching the gospel, especially the persecution from his own kinsmen. One explanation says the thorn must have been sexual temptation because that is the last instinct monks are able to conquer in their ascetic life.

Whatever it was, Paul's reaction wasn't, "Well, this has happened to me so I will just try to get along somehow." Rather, he asked the Lord to remove it.

Instead of removing it, the Lord said, "My grace is sufficient for thee: for my strength is made perfect in weakness" (2 Cor. 12:9). The answer was so clear that Paul saw no need in asking again.

For someone who would have to continue bearing a thorn as difficult as malaria or persecution, Paul made a startling response to the Lord's answer. One translation says Paul boasted about his weaknesses, for he was well content with them. Another said he delighted in them, for he was glad to suffer for Christ's sake.

Considering Paul's response, does it sound as though he regarded the thorn as a tragedy? Did he regard the Lord's answer as a tragedy? No, Paul did not; but there is a tragedy involved here, and that tragedy is the way we've interpreted Paul's experience with regard to prayer. We've abused Paul's experience by thinking the no answer meant it was wrong of Paul to have asked.

What we are really saying is that a no answer indicates we should never have asked in the first place. One old but still widely circulated book of prayer asks, How could Paul, who had the mind of Christ, make such a request? Having the mind of Christ (1 Cor. 2:16) is the reason why Paul knew he could and should ask. Paul may very well have remembered Jesus' praying three times for the cup of suffering to be removed from him. He remembered that, following prayer, Jesus went bravely forth to the task before him.

On other occasions, Jesus withdrew from the crowds to pray and be alone with God. Prayer refreshed him and strengthened him. Likewise, on the night he was to be betrayed, on the eve of when he would come to trial and then face death, Jesus asked for a way of escape. When he asked, Jesus gave God the channel needed to provide the strength for what must be done. Even while Jesus was praying, Luke says, an angel came to strengthen him (22:43).

One of Paul's favorite expressions was "in Christ." Paul knew the name of Jesus; he knew his character and nature. Paul so identified with Christ that in his moment of great affliction, he knew that it was right to ask for the thorn to be removed.

In addition, we've abused Paul's experience by accepting the answer he received without having made his request. One housewife who regards her children as thorns in the flesh said her favorite Bible verse is 2 Corinthians 12:9. "When my house is a wreck, my husband due home in an hour, dinner unprepared and the beds still unmade, and the children screaming at each other," she said, "I just remember what the Lord said to Paul, that his grace would be sufficient." No one in her prayer group had the nerve to tell her that grace wasn't what she needed. A little organization early in the morning before the "thorns" got up would help a lot more.

A bit more serious is the woman who stopped by to tell me of her impending operation. Although the operation had been in consideration for some time, the doctor's final word had left her visibly shaken. As if she were trying to summon all of her courage, she heaved a big sigh and said, "I just have to accept this as God's will for me. I guess he intended a life of suffering for me."

Anyone is bound to say something like that under stress, so I was careful to be gentle with my inquiry. "Have you asked God to heal you?"

"No, I haven't," was her reply. "I just figured God wanted this for me. That it was his plan."

"How can you assume it is God's will until you have asked him to heal you? Maybe this is a time for God to receive glory, not a time for you to suffer. Asking will let you know."

When Jesus heard that Lazarus was sick, he said, "The final result of this sickness will not be the death of Lazarus; this has happened to bring glory to God, and will be the means by which the Son of God will receive glory" (John 11:4, TEV).

To not ask is to not give God the channel he needs to perform a glorious work in our lives. To not ask is to do God a disservice, for it might be the very opportunity he needs to bring honor and glory upon his name. When we have asked and have understood God to say no, we can proceed in the certainty that what we are suffering is God's will for us. It is at this point that we can accept Paul's answer for our situation. If God does not alter our course, he will give us grace to face it as he did Paul and as he did Jesus. The grace will be so sufficient that we'll be able to say with Paul, "I am content" (2 Cor. 12:10, TEV). We can have that kind of reaction when we've given God the channel he needs to supply us with sufficient grace.

Paul's experience encourages us to approach God. Notice the name by which he addressed God. Paul called him "Lord." Remembering the suffering and humiliation Jesus experienced, Paul prayed to him. Paul was not trying to separate the Trinity. Indeed, Paul recognized the greatness and completeness of God; but on this occasion, he addressed the suffering nature of God as seen in Jesus.

Paul's experience gives us confidence in the rightness to ask. As Christians, we should never let it be said about us that we have not for we ask not. As we grow in faith, we open ourselves to God to allow him to do all he wills to do through us. To not ask is to leave areas of our lives closed off to him and limits what he can do.

Paul's experience reminds us of God's mercifulness in answering. Some Christians hold up three fingers and strongly pronounce, "Three times Paul asked," as if that were really something. Their implication is, Look at Paul; look at who he was; and look at the fact that he went before God three times to try to get what he wanted.

Those three times in asking might have all been in the same prayer, just as Jesus' thrice-placed request in the garden of Gethsemane. Paul could have mentioned the three times to show us that God responded with such surety that Paul knew the matter was settled and he did not need to ask again. God's quick response showed Paul what course of action he was to take and did not leave him in doubt concerning God's will.

On the other hand, what if Paul mentioned the three times to show the agony of his need? Begging would seem like a most natural reaction for someone in the stress of high fever or dangerous persecution. He poured out his heart to the Lord. Paul, the one who taught us that the Holy Spirit aids in our praying, knew that he could. He knew that he could plead without bargaining and without offering conditions. He did not hesitate to ask out of fear that something worse, more grotesque than what he was already experiencing, would happen to him. He knew the Lord as someone to be trusted.

For some reason, God chose not to remove Paul's thorn. Paul said it was to keep him from being puffed up. Whatever the reason, God did not leave Paul to handle it alone. God answers mercifully; he gave Paul the grace to live with it.

God's heart is touched by the infirmities of his children, those within and those without the fold. The merciful answers that he gives are continually underscored for us when we interact and pray with others. They are verified by the Bible and by our experience when properly interpreted. Shouldn't we ask, then, of the one who answers so graciously and mercifully?

To not ask is to indicate distrust.

To not ask is to say to God, I don't believe you are who you say you are.

To not ask is to withhold from God an opportunity to do with and through us what he could never do to us or against us.

To not ask is to miss out on joy—the joy that bubbles right up to the brim of our cup when God repeatedly answers and responds to us.

So let's ask, that our joy may be full and that we can give God the regard which he so rightfully deserves.